DUMP TRUCKS

DONALD F. WOOD

Dedication

To Beverley and Bert Prouty—"sparkplugs" for truck historians in central California.

First published in 2001 by MBI Publishing Company, 729 Prospect Avenue, PO Box 1, Osceola, WI 54020-0001 USA

MBI Publishing Company books are also available at discounts in bulk quantity for industrial or sales-promotional use. For details write to Special Sales Manager at Motorbooks International Wholesalers & Distributors, 729 Prospect Avenue, PO Box 1, Osceola, WI 54020-0001 USA.

On the front cover: Upper left: A 1917 GMC. *GMC* *Upper right:* A 1939 White used by the Great Lakes Coal and Dock Company, in Milwaukee. *Great Lakes Coal & Dock Co.* *Lower left:* A 1945 International K-3 with a Marion 2-yard dump body. *Kranz-built Bodies* *Lower right:* An early 1990s Freightliner with a Fontaine dump body. *Freightliner*

On the back cover: Top: A 1920 Acason truck with a Fruehauf semitrailer that dumps. *Fruehauf* *Middle:* A Mack off-highway earth mover called the 'Mack Pack'. *Mack Trucks* *Bottom:* A mid-1970s Ford with a Peabody Galion body, dual axles, and a cab protector. *Peabody Galion*

Library of Congress Cataloging-in-Publication Data
Wood, Donald F.
    Dump Trucks / Donald F. Wood.
       p. cm. — (The Crestline series)
    Includes index.
    ISBN 0-7603-0867-5 (pbk. : alk. paper)
    1. Dump trucks—History. I. Title. II. Series.

TL230.5D85 W66   2001
629.225—dc21   00-060093

Layout by Terry Webster and LeAnn Kuhlmann
Cover by Tom Heffron

Printed in the United States of America

Contents

Preface

A number of individuals assisted in the preparation of this book. They include Mark Anthony; Gary M. Callis; James R. Duclon; Allen M. Fisher; Al Garcia; Dave Gitchell, W. S. Darley & Co.; Robert V. Hinshaw, The Truck Engineering Company, Inc.; Peter D. Jones, Crysteel Mfg. Inc.; John Miller; Chuck Rhoads; Charles F. Risley; Thomas F. Root; Ron Sperry; E. R. "Gus" St. Marie, Reliance Heavy Duty Trailers; John C. Steighner; and G. Thiele, Thiele Industries, Inc.

Several persons generously contribute to a fund at San Francisco State University that supports old truck research. We acknowledge some of the donors: Phillip Baumgarten, Edward C. Couderc of Sausalito Moving & Storage, Gilbert Hall, David Kiely, ROADSHOW, Gene Olson, Oshkosh Truck Foundation, Alvin Shaw, Art Van Aken, Charlie Wacker, Bill West, and Fred Woods. Several chapters of the American Truck Historical Society have helped, including Black Swamp, Central Coast of California, Hiawathaland, Inland Empire, Mason-Dixon, Metro Jersey, Minnesota Metro, Music City, Northeast Ohio, Shenandoah Valley, South Florida, and Southern Michigan.

Introduction

A common body on heavy trucks is the "dump" body, which usually raises in the front, dumping the body's contents to the rear. A second form of dump body is a hopper that empties through the bottom. Since about the time of World War II, some very large dump trucks have been developed for use in off-highway situations, usually strip mining, major road building, or other construction. While most dump bodies dump toward the rear of the truck, some dump toward either side.

Dump trucks and dump bodies are measured in different ways. Weights, like 2 or 5 tons, relate to the truck, its tires, frame, and suspension and overall ability to support heavy loads. Many dump bodies are referred to by their capacity in yards, meaning cubic yards. The practice of selling loads by volume arises because material weights typically change with moisture content—goods exposed to rain will weigh more than an equal volume of the material stored indoors. Hence one buys *yards* of sand or gravel. Dump bodies are given two cubic-yard capacities, one for the material filled level with the top of the sideboards, and another with the material piled up. The capacity in the first instance is called "water level" or yards level; capacity with the load piled up is called yards "heaped." Sometimes dump bodies are referred to in feet, and that is usually their horizontal length measured along the side of the truck.

The term "pup" is applied to several styles of trailers, usually self-supporting on two axles with a long drawbar—because of axle weight and spacing regulations. Most look as though they would carry about as much as a dump body on a conventional two-axle straight-frame truck chassis. Most pup trucks are equipped with hoists—with hydraulic and air hoses leading along the drawbar to the truck. When a regular dump truck pulls a pup, unloading controls for both loads are in the truck's cab. The driver can either back with the trailer at a 90-degree angle and dump both loads, or dump the truck's load over the drawbar.

Another form of trailer is called the "transfer" trailer. The dump box on the transfer trailer is slightly smaller than the dump box on the truck that's pulling it. The box on the transfer trailer rides on two rails, about 34 inches apart. After the truck dumps its load, it reconnects to the trailer, dropping the drawbar and drawing the trailer right next to the truck. The trailer's box is then moved into the truck's box and locked into place. The truck's dumping mechanism is used to dump the trailer's box.

This book includes numerous photos, from many states. Individuals who read credit lines will see that we relied on many different batches, each from a different time period. We have no single source that covers the entire century. Most of the technological development of dump bodies had taken place by the 1930s and trucks were nearly fully developed by 1940. The major change since then has been that the rigs in use have been getting larger and larger. One reason that dump trucks look different is that each state maintains its own controls on axle weights and spacing. Dump trucks are almost always at or near their weight limit. The term "bridge formula" describes the state's axle weight and spacing rules and their application. Virtually every dump truck buyer takes these rules into account.

Chapter 1

1901–1910

Trucks, the First Decade

The motor truck came into use during this first decade of the twentieth century. Many were offshoots of autos but others were specially developed to handle heavy loads. Toward the end of the decade, a few industrial operations began using very large trucks with dump bodies. Most carried coal. It's difficult today to realize how important coal was 100 years ago. It was used to heat nearly all buildings in urban areas and to provide steam for powering industrial plants and generating electricity. Coal was consumed in great quantities by railroad locomotives and many ships and boats. Burning coal also produced large quantities of cinders and ashes that had to be hauled away.

Prior to the motor truck, horse- and mule-drawn rigs were used to haul and "dump" materials. Two-wheel carts had the body hinged to the axle with the center of gravity, when loaded, just behind the axle. The loaded body was kept hooked at the front and, when unhooked, would dump. In open mines, horses or mules would pull strings of cars, which typically opened to the side, along rail track. Often the track led to a raised platform above open rail cars, where the materials would be dumped and then carried off by rail. Just after 1900 there were also some four-wheel horse-drawn flatbed wagons that carried a rectangular body, lifted by a hand hoist in the front.

The Anthony Company, engaged in a patent suit, prepared a booklet in 1931 entitled *A Pictorial History of Vehicle Dump Bodies.* This picture appeared in the book; it shows a 5-ton Robertson Steam Wagon, built in England and equipped with one of the earliest hydraulic dumping mechanisms. *Mark Anthony*

The Anthony Company, a dump truck body builder, was engaged in a patent suit in 1931. At that time, it released a publication, *A Pictorial History of Vehicle Dump Bodies*, which contained pictures of early equipment. Some of the early vehicles in the book included a Mann gravity dump, built in England in 1904, and a Bristol dump body, which was raised manually with a continuous screw hoist, built in England in 1905. The first hydraulic hoist was on a Robertson Steam Wagon, built in England in 1904 or 1905. The hydraulic hoist received its power from either of two sources: the truck's engine or an independent steam engine. In 1907 the Glasgow firm of Alley & MacLellan developed a body that used a "tipping cylinder" at the bottom of the body and parallel to the truck. Water would be pumped back or forth to tip or to restore the body to a level position. Ernest Sternberg's *A History of Motor Truck Development* contains a picture of a 1909 dump truck with Spanish lettering on the side. The body was lifted by a hand hoist.

Some of the earliest truck-mounted dump bodies relied on gravity. The body pivoted off-center and, when level, was locked in place. When the lock was released, the body would dump toward the rear. The

The Anthony booklet showed this hand-operated hydraulic hoist, used in the United States for unloading grain from a farm wagon. *Mark Anthony*

Another early hydraulic dump was developed by Alley & MacLellan of Glasgow, in about 1907. This picture appeared in the Anthony booklet. The truck was powered by steam. *Mark Anthony*

body was shaped and placed so that when empty it would ride in the nondumping position. It had to be locked into this position because, once loaded, its center of gravity would shift rearward, causing it to dump. Once empty, the box would move forward on its own. This style of dump body had some limitation if the haul were of any length because the weight of the load would fall near or behind the rear axle, which produced poor weight distribution over the entire chassis.

There were also bottom-dump trailers mounted between two axles, and pulled by horses. The body would be two halves, each mounted on a hinge. The two sides would be drawn together by chains and tightened with a ratchet. When the operator was ready to dump, he or she would depress a foot pedal that released the ratchet, allowing the two body halves to spread.

Another mechanical dump shown in the Anthony booklet was the Mann steam truck from England. This was a gravity dump. *Mark Anthony*

Chutes on the sides of this trailer body are used to empty the coal. The tractor is a 1910 Couple Gear, built in Grand Rapids, Michigan. At this time the firm was building both electric and gas-electric trucks. (Gas-electric trucks used gasoline engines to generate electricity to power the wheels, similar to the diesel train engines of today.) *National Automotive History Collection, Detroit Public Library*

This is a circa 1910 Lauth-Juergens, with what looks like a mechanically raised dump body. Lauth-Juergens trucks were built in Fremont, Ohio. Today the firm is best known to truck historians as the place where Magnus Hendrickson, of Hendrickson truck fame, got his start. *Hendrickson Mfg. Co.*

The name "Pope" can be seen on this circa 1910 truck's radiator. It's probably a Pope-Hartford. The body is shaped to discharge coal through chutes at the bottom. *The William F. Harrah Automobile Foundation*

Chapter 2

1911–1920

Dump Trucks Become Indispensible

In the second decade of the twentieth century, the motor truck came into widespread use. For dumping operations, the motor truck was vastly superior to systems utilizing horses or mules. Many dump body builders appeared, and they would sell the body and hoist to be attached to a chassis such as a Ford, Reo, or Mack. World War I demonstrated the superiority of the motor truck in many challenging situations. Meeting wartime orders also helped truck manufacturers improve product quality, and military service trained many men to drive trucks.

The earliest U.S. developments of dump bodies shown in the Anthony booklet mentioned in the previous chapter were a 1911 Gramm that used a mechanical hoist connected to a power take-off (PTO), and a 1911 Sampson that had a vertical hydraulic hoist, also powered by the truck's motor. Also pictured was a 1912 White with a hand-hoist dump body.

An early article about dump trucks appeared in a 1912 issue of *The Motor Truck*. It dealt with the use of electric trucks to haul coal in the Boston area. Most of the article was devoted to comparing the costs of hauling

This is a 1911 Avery, built in Peoria, Illinois. The firm also built farm tractors. The body appears to rely on gravity to be dumped; at least a third of it rides behind the frame. At the front, note that the steering wheel is on this side of the hood. It's difficult to discern how the lifting mechanism was powered, or how the driver steered. *The William F. Harrah Automobile Foundation*

by horse with those of electric trucks. At the time, nine firms in the area were operating a total of 16 electric trucks for deliveries, and had another 8 units on order. The electric trucks were built by three firms: Couple Gear Freight-Wheel Company, Eldridge, and General Vehicle Company.

A firm in Brookline used a Couple Gear tractor to pull a wagon carrying 3 tons of coal. The body had a "dumping installation" and several steering wheel-sized gear wheels on the side—although one cannot tell whether they lifted the body or merely chute doors, allowing gravity to unload the coal into baskets. The second example, an Eldridge 5-ton tip cart, was a straight frame truck. The front wheels were powered by Couple Gear electric motors, with the batteries under the driver's seat. The dump body was centered just ahead of the rear axle and what appears to be a hand hoist lifted it from the front. A third example dealt with a truck (chassis maker unspecified) that used an electric hoist. "This was the first electrically hoisted tip cart ever built…" The article also mentioned other coal units

Sauer trucks were built in Europe and briefly sold in the United States by a firm that ultimately became Mack. This 1912 Sauer was used by a Long Island coal dealer. The driver lifts the body by using the crank. *American Truck Historical Society*

Commer trucks were built in England and imported into the United States, where their assembly was completed. This movement ended when England became involved in World War I. This 1912 Commer has right-hand steering. Note hand-brake lever and cable. Body unloads through side chutes. It's not clear from the photo whether it lifts. *National Automotive History Collection, Detroit Public Library*

Speedwell trucks were built in Dayton from 1907 until 1915. This one found its way west to Klamath Falls, Oregon. The body is lifted by a hand-cranked hoist. Note the horn and foot lever outside the body. *Klamath County Museum*

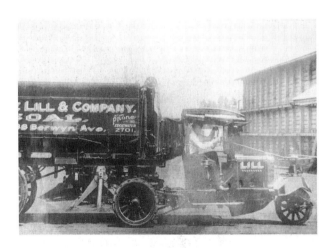

Before World War I, Knox-Martin built three-wheel tractors with chain-driven rear wheels. This one pulled a large dump trailer, lifted by a vertical hoist. *Press Tank & Equipment Co., Chicago*

that were on order. One was to be "equipped with a Keystone hoist," and another "will have a dumping body with a chain hoist."

A 1918 book by S. V. Norton, *The Motor Truck as an Aid to Business Profits*, contained a chapter entitled "Helping the Truck To Unload Effectively." Truck operators wanted rapid unloading, since this would reduce the truck's turn-around time, allowing it to make more trips in a given time period. Norton discusses two types of dump bodies: the common type with the body hinged at the rear of the frame, and the elevated body (generally used for coal), with struts and beams underneath in a scissors arrangement that elevated the body when the beams were pulled closer together. (Sometimes while elevating, the hopper's front would be raised higher so that it would be ready to empty out of the rear.) These elevated dumping bodies were used mainly for delivering coal. (Later, concrete mixers would also be elevated.) The purpose of the elevation was to allow the materials to flow by gravity along chutes for some distance from the truck. In addition to scissors-like lifts, a few coal bodies were elevated by four screws, one in each corner, powered by the truck's PTO. Gravity pitch would be built into the body so that coal would feed out of the hopper and into the chute. A gate at the bottom of the hopper would control the outward flow of coal. Even if chutes could not

continued on page 16

A circa 1913 Moreland used in Santa Barbara. The dump body is lifted by a vertical hoist. Note the spout in front of the cargo box, apparently to feed a stream of gravel along the road's shoulder. Morelands were built in Los Angeles between 1911 and 1941. *Library, Univ. of California, Los Angeles*

Pope-Hartford trucks were made in Hartford, Connecticut, from 1906 until 1914. The dump body on this one appears to be lifted manually by the hand crank, visible above the chain drive. *The William F. Harrah Automobile Foundation*

Here are four pre-World War I Locomobiles used by the U.S. Army Corps of Engineers in Southern California. *U.S. Army Corps of Engineers, Los Angeles District*

Blair trucks were built in Newark, Ohio, between 1911 and 1918. In total, only 25 were built. The trucks were some of the earliest users of worm drive. The sign on the side of the dump box says, "Blair Direct worm drive pneumatic dumping car, River Sand Company, Niagara Falls, New York." *The Smithsonian Institution*

A fleet of four circa 1915 Garford coal trucks. Garford trucks were built in Ohio from 1908 until 1933. *Press Tank & Equipment Co., Chicago*

A circa 1915 White with steel wheels pulling two trailers. At the front of the rear trailer a hoisting device is visible. *Volvo/White*

Dart trucks were built throughout most of the twentieth century; the firm is now part of Paccar. This Dart, from about 1915, has a vertical hydraulic hoist to lift its dump body. *The Smithsonian Institution*

This is a circa 1915 Wichita truck photographed in San Francisco. Stenciling on the side of the dump body says: "Lowney's Practical Dump Body Apparatus." Wichita trucks were made in Wichita Falls, Texas, between 1911 and 1932. *Railway Negative Exchange*

Gersix trucks were built in the Pacific Northwest; the firm eventually became Kenworth. This is a 1915 Gersix with a dump body. (The white in the background was retouched so picture could be used in an ad.) *American Automobile Manufacturers Assn.*

Here's a pair of World War I-era Garford dump trucks at work in Chicago, with a steam shovel in the background. *Press Tank & Equipment Co., Chicago*

Continued from page 12

be used, the body was often elevated so that the baskets would be loaded at shoulder height, and the workers could grab them at that height and avoid lifting them, saving time (and backs).

Norton's book also discussed mounting cranes on trucks to load or unload bulk materials. Usually these would be used on one-time pickup or delivery situations where regular material-handling equipment was not already available.

Some bodies were constructed with pitch built into the floor. The operator needed only to open gates in the bottom to allow materials to flow out. The amount of pitch was based on the material's "angle of repose," which is the angle the surface of the pile makes when loose material is piled freely. The flatter the pile, the lower the material's angle of repose. The body's floor must be pitched at a steeper angle than the material's angle of repose if the material is to flow freely out of the hopper. Coke has an angle of repose of 23 degrees, while soft coal's angle of repose is 30 degrees.

Early dumping vehicles faced additional challenges when hauling bricks. If dumped freely, many bricks

would break. Bricks therefore required special bodies. Some were designed so that when the dump body was raised, its rear end would be only a few inches above the ground. The driver would then pull away slowly, letting the load slip off the truck, rather than cascade and tumble harshly onto the ground. The second method was to use a body that would slide completely off the truck frame and rest at a 90 degree angle on the ground. This system set the load of bricks on the ground. The operator could then pick up the body later, once the bricks were removed. Since the body was removable, the brick kiln would own several and would be filling some while the trucks were making deliveries with the others.

Norton's book had pictures of some dump bodies with multiple hoppers. They were generally used by coal yards, with each hopper containing coal for an individual customer. Another way of dealing with this was to place dividers inside a dump body, with the load for the first customer placed closest to the rear. Companies also used four-wheel dump trailers that emptied through the bottom. Several of these trailers could be pulled by trucks with low gear ratios—this was before the time when states began imposing weight and length limits on trucks and truck trailers. There were also no height limits, and many of the bodies seem high by today's standards. They were built higher to create the height and pitch needed for easy unloading. These rigs were so slow that going around a curve with a high center of gravity was not an issue.

Some bodies dumped manually, either with a mechanical or, later, a hydraulic hoist. On these bodies, the pivot point was moved forward, so the operator needed to lift only the difference in weight between the load forward and rear of the balance point.

A 1919 article on truck bodies from *The Commercial Car Journal* described many new body styles and

A 1915–1916 White tractor pulling a "Bull Dog" bottom-dumping trailer, built in Kansas City, Missouri, and used for spreading gravel. *Volvo/White*

Wilcox trucks were made in Minneapolis from 1910 until 1927. This one, from about 1916, has a vertical hydraulic hoist, shown in both lowered and raised position. Braces connected to the frame in front of the rear axel keep the raised body from moving left or right. *National Automotive History Collection, Detroit Public Library*

A circa 1916 Knox tractor with a semitrailer lifted by vertical hydraulic hoists. The full trailer to the rear appears to dump toward the sides. Detroit Trailer Co. supplied some of the equipment shown. *Whitehead & Kales, Detroit*

included photographs. Some of the designs are summarized below:

- Seven dump body styles were built by the Kilbourne & Jacobs Manufacturing Company of Columbus, Ohio. One body was asbestos lined and intended for carrying hot asphalt. Another could have sideboards, tailgate, and rear stakes removed so it could function as a flatbed. A garbage body was sealed at the bottom to keep liquids from dripping. Another dump model had a double-action tailgate. When hinged at the top, it would allow for a direct dump and when hinged from the bottom, it would allow workers to unload by hand or by using shovels. Lastly, a coal-handling body had a small door in the tailgate and hooks for baskets.

- The Simplex Manufacturing Company of Conneautville, Pennsylvania, offered several bodies that were lifted by a vertical hand hoist. The hoist, which occupied only 9 inches of space in front of the body, was geared so the operator's effort was multiplied by a factor of 80.

- The Metropolitan Body Company of Bridgeport, Connecticut, offered a "combination" body in two sizes. "Combination" meant that, in addition to serving as a dump truck, its sides could be removed for use as a flatbed, or stakes could be added for carrying general freight.

- The Wood Hydraulic Hoist and Body Company of Detroit offered its single-piston vertical hoist. The makers state that "with a Wood hoist it is possible to dump a capacity load in 15 seconds. After the commodity has been dumped, the driver can start immediately without waiting for the body to come back down into position. This seems a small item, but in figuring the cost of a job, every minute counts."

- A coal body was pictured on an Armleder truck (with the body builder unspecified). The body had a false floor slanting downward to the rear so coal would slide out by gravity through chutes to baskets on the rear platform. The rear platform, which looked like a tailgate, could then be elevated using the truck's power (like the powered liftgates

A 1917 GMC making a coal delivery. When the body was level, it was still relatively high, but that made it easier for the driver and his helper to haul coal by the basket—the baskets would be at shoulder height. *GMC*

of today) but to shoulder height, saving the workers from having to lift the filled baskets.

- A short body for dumping bricks, built by the American Truck and Body Company of Martinsville, Virginia, also was shown.

- The Federal Motor Company, a truck builder, apparently had a body department that designed a removable dump body. When removed, the body would be stored on a stand of chassis height. The same rollers that allowed the body to be slid on and off could also be used for handling other heavy items—such as lumber—after the dump body had been removed.

- Autocar, another truck builder, also had a "body designing department." It offered several factory-installed dump bodies, including a high-lift, power-operated, coal chute body that sold for $650.

- Lee Loader & Body Company built a four-body unit mounted on a truck trailer. Each body unit, with a 1-yard capacity, could be dumped to the right or to the left.

- The Archer Iron Works of Chicago offered eight sizes of dump bodies, all lifted with hand-operated hoists. The company's smallest unit was intended solely for Fords.

- Also shown in the article were dump bodies built by Duplex Truck Company, Lansing, Michigan; Horizontal Hydraulic Hoist Company, Detroit, Michigan; and Providence Body Co., Providence, Rhode Island.

A number of ads for dump bodies appeared in the same issue, including one by the Metropolitan Body Company for its "combination" body described above. Simplex advertised its combination body by urging, "You cannot afford to handicap your truck with a body capable of only one line of service. It must be equipped to meet every need which arises." This message was probably directed at freight haulers, who couldn't be sure at the time they purchased their vehicle what types of freight they might be asked to haul. The Daily Motor Truck Bodies firm of Chicago advertised both dump bodies and hand hoists. Auto Truck Steel Body Co. of Chicago offered dump bodies ranging from 2 to 6 tons in capacity, and one is shown to be raised by a vertical hydraulic hoist. The Woonsocket Wagon Manufacturing Company of Woonsocket, Rhode Island, advertised a steel dump body mounted on a semitrailer and lifted

continued on page 22

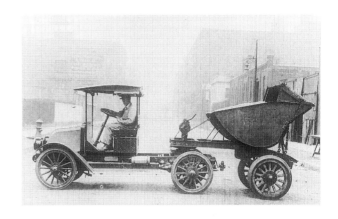

Three views of a gravity dump body pulled by a circa 1917 International tractor. The load was about a yard of gravel. Noted vehicle historian Fred Crismon, who wrote *International Trucks*, said that these were the earliest pictures of International trucks employing fifth-wheel trailer connections. *Navistar Archives*

A 1917 Mack Bulldog pulling a dumping semitrailer. *Mack Museum*

Close-up shows mechanical lifting device that rides above the fifth wheel. We are unable to tell how it was powered. *Mack Museum*

Riker trucks were built by Locomobile, and this one apparently has the word "Locomobile" on its side. The truck has a hydraulic piston hoist and was owned by the City of Duluth. *National Automotive History Collection, Detroit Public Library*

A Corbitt from the late teens, with a body that dumps to either side. Corbitt trucks were built in Henderson, North Carolina, between 1915 and 1958. *American Truck Historical Society*

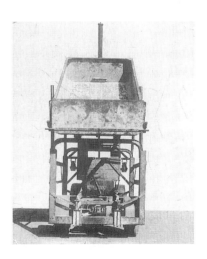

Gramm-Bernstein trucks were made in Lima, Ohio. This one has a Heil twin-piston underbody hydraulic hoist. Heil advertised that its twin-piston hoists had a compensating movement of the hoist pistons that allowed one to rise faster until the load on both was equalized. A sign at top center of the windshield says "Ship by Truck," a World War I program aimed at reducing railroad congestion. *The Heil Co.*

The number "17" shows on the license plate. This is the rear view of a body that apparently is lifted by continuous screws in each corner, and then dumps. Note height of the hoist in top center of picture. *Auto Truck*

Continued from page 19

with a hand hoist. Littleford Bros. of Cincinnati advertised steel dump bodies. The most unusual dump body advertised was built by Lawrence Bruder of Cincinnati. Just forward of the truck's rear axle was a turntable, set on roller bearings. Attached to the turntable was a long frame that carried both a dump body and its mechanical, hand-cranked hoist. The turntable thus allowed the load to be dumped at any spot along a 180-degree arc.

At the end of World War I, the U.S. Army gave thousands of surplus military trucks to state highway departments for use in highway construction and maintenance. The total is not known, but it must have been large, since at least 5,000 FWDs alone were distributed. Indiana received 88 surplus FWDs, and had the metal

ammunition bodies cut down to 2-1/2 yard capacity, and then turned them into dump trucks by adding hydraulic cable hoists in the front. Highway building in the early 1920s brought about the development of a specialized dump body used for carrying wet concrete short distances to where it was needed. (This was before the development of the "cement mixer" with agitators that kept the load from settling.) If a highway were being paved, the construction crew would build a temporary mixing plant, which they would have to move every few days. A large fleet of small trucks carried the wet concrete in gravity-dump hoppers. A Packard brochure of the time contained a table showing the number of trucks that would be needed to deliver 40 batches of wet concrete per hour. The table covered hauling distances from 1/4 mile to 6 miles, one way, and assumed an average truck speed of 10 to 25 miles per hour. The number of trucks required ranged from 4 to 52.

The Firestone Tire Company began a campaign to increase truck use for short hauls and also to improve the nation's road system. In 1920, Firestone issued a number of publications dealing with industries in which truck use was increasing. One Firestone report featured open coal mines, in which trucks were replacing horses in hauling the mined coal to a railhead. The authors of the report had difficulty finding operators who kept good financial records, so they were unable to make any truck/horse comparisons. They did publish the costs for a truck operator who carried 6-1/2 ton loads of coal for 9 miles and then returned empty. This trucker traveled about 16,000 miles per year at a cost of

A cumbersome dumping mechanism on a World War I vintage Mack carrying bagged coal. *Mack Museum*

Mechanically astute readers will have to figure out exactly how it works. *Mack Museum*

During World War I, the U.S. government wrote specifications for "standardized" trucks for use by the military. These truck makes were generally referred to as "USA" or "Liberty." At the war's end, large numbers were given to state highway departments for use in road construction and maintenance. This surplus Liberty truck was given to California. *CALTRANS Photo Archives*

44 cents per truck mile. Here's the cost breakdown per ton mile in cents: gasoline, 7.98; grease, 0.36; oil, 0.73; machinery, 3.04; battery, 0.07; body, 2.03; tires, 3.98; sundries, 2.69; operator, 12.37; helper, 0.54; garage, 0.55; depreciation, 6.23; interest, 1.94; fire insurance, 0.14; liability insurance, 1.28; and, license, 0.17. The truck averaged 3.37 miles per gallon of gasoline, and 72.01 miles per gallon of oil, which says something about oil consumption in circa 1920 motors. The report said that these costs were atypical because the haul in question involved moving coal to a lower elevation, hence the loaded truck was traveling downhill and returning empty going uphill.

Packard Motor Car Company offered various hoists and dump bodies that could be installed on its trucks at the factory. They were built by the Horizontal Hydraulic Hoist Company. Three hoists and four bodies were offered. A PTO adaptation, which came off of the truck's transmission, was $85; installing the hoist was $40; and installing both the hoist and body was $60. Prices of bodies with hoists ranged from $900 to $1,180. Customers could also order a dump frame with hoist and install their own choice of body. Twelve combinations of hoist capacities and body frame lengths were available. Five of the frames were 6 inches wider at the back than the front, which complemented bodies that were wider toward the bottom. Increased width near the bottom of the body allowed materials to flow more easily. The booklet also contained instructions for hoist care:

The hoist cylinder should be filled with oil every two months. This is done by raising the body and blocking it up at the highest angle to permit lowering of the hoist arms. When the hoist arms are at their lowest point, the piston rod is forced into the cylinder as far as it will go. Remove all three plugs on

A late-teens Nash Quad used by the Wisconsin Highway Commission. It has a Heil hydraulic dump body. Note crossed cables or narrow bars. Their function may have been to hold an empty body in an upright position for a period of time. *The Heil Co.*

Loading gravel into a White at the time of World War I. Silos behind the truck are filled by a scoop that unloads rail cars in the background. *Volvo/White*

The Velie Motor Vehicle Co. of Moline, Illinois, built this truck for the U.S. Army during World War I. A Dailey hand-raised hoist (manufactured in Chicago) was used to lift the dump body. *Auto Truck*

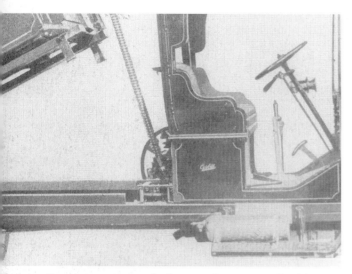

Continuous screw hoist on a late-teens Corbitt. *American Truck Historical Society*

Lapeer built truck tractors from 1916 until 1920. This rig is pulling a coal trailer that was probably hoisted using manual equipment. Framework below the truck has a scissors-jack appearance. *Roger Bros., Albion, Pennsylvania*

the top of the hoist cylinder and pour the oil through the 3/4-inch opening until it runs out of one of the smaller openings, and then replace plugs. Elevate hoist until lifting arms come in contact with body, taking load off the blocks, and then remove blocks.

In summer, use steam cylinder oil thinned slightly with kerosene so that it will flow slowly. For moderately cold weather use more kerosene; for extreme cold use ice machine oil.

This is from a 1919 Hahn brochure, which said that at full height, coal could "shoot" 44 feet. Hahn trucks were built in Hamburg, Pennsylvania. The firm is known best for its line of fire apparatus. *The Smithsonian Institution*

This is a street cleaning body, made at the Sing Sing prison. It's shown in a position to dump the debris it has gathered. Note geared mechanism by rear wheel.

This truck was used to build roads in California just after World War I. Note how it's being loaded. The horse above has dragged a scraper full of gravel over a grilled trap above the truck. Barely visible above the scraper, we see some cables rigged to the scraper. The operator pulls on one to trip a lever that tips the scraper so that the smooth rounded portion is dragged over the grate, rather than the blade, which would damage the grate. *California State Archives*

A late-teens White with a dump body with vertical hoist installed by the S. S. Albright Company, of Sacramento. *California State Library*

Standard trucks were produced in Detroit. This circa 1919 model has a dump body with the vertical hoist barely visible behind the truck's cab. Note rolled-up side curtains. *Oregon Historical Society*

Here's a late-teens Winther, built in Kenosha, Wisconsin, with an Auto Truck-installed body. The Auto Truck firm was, and is, located in the Chicago area. *Auto Truck*

A turntable is under construction in the middle of a roadway. Wet concrete-carrying trucks, circa 1920 Autocars, have driven up from the right and, at the turntable, are turned around. They then back and queue in front of the pavement-spreading device, barely visible in the background. *Portland Cement Association*

This Autocar has reached the pavement-laying machine. It will dump its load into the machine's bucket and return for another load. The fresh pavement is being spread to the rear of the photo. *Portland Cement Association*

The United States Motor Truck Co., of Cincinnati, turned out trucks from 1909 until 1930. This model, from about 1920, carries a mechanically hoisted, 3-1/2-cubic-yard Highway body. *Dorsey Trailers, Edgerton, Wisconsin*

This is a 1920 Available truck with solid tires and a dump body. Availables were built in Chicago from 1910 until the mid-1950s. *Free Library of Philadelphia*

Fageols were a well-known Western truck, built in Oakland, California. They are easily recognized because of their shark-fin cooling vents on top of the hood. Here's a circa 1920 Fageol used in San Mateo County, just south of San Francisco. The two-piston hydraulic dump body was built by Heil. *The Heil Co.*

A hand-cranked dump body under construction, circa 1920. It will be attached to the truck's frame. Note metal U-bolts in foreground. *National Automotive History Collection, Detroit Public Library*

A Moreland tractor, from about 1920, pulling a long dump trailer lifted by a vertical hydraulic hoist. *Library, Univ. of California, Los Angeles*

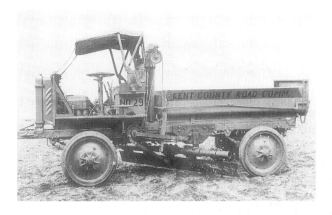

A circa 1920 Nash Quad with a dump body with a vertical hoist, operated by the Kent County Highway Commission. Beneath the truck is mounted a Monarch scraper blade. *Monarch Road Machinery Co.*

Hendrickson trucks were built in the Chicago area for much of the twentieth century. This 1920 model has a dump body lifted by a hand-cranked hoist at the front. *Hendrickson Mfg. Co.*

A circa 1920 Autocar with a Heil scissors-lift coal body.
The Heil Co.

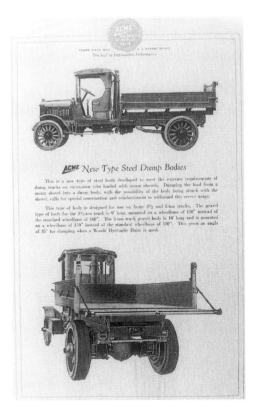

Page from a 1920 Acme truck brochure showing gravel dump bodies. They could dump at a 35-degree angle when a Wood hoist was used. *Free Library of Philadelphia*

Hand crank and hoist on a dump body mounted on a 1920 Ford owned by Carl Liranzo.

Chapter 3
1921–1930

A Decade of Innovations

The 1920s were prosperous. The economy boomed and dump trucks were needed to serve the building and construction industries. The many developments and improvements in trucks during this period included four-wheel hydraulic brakes, as well as air brakes and dual-powered rear axles. Many trucks had cabs, windshields, and windshield wipers. Some aluminum was used. Over the decade, trucks switched from solid to pneumatic tires. Concrete mixers were introduced and would do away with the "batch" trucks.

Victor Page's book, *The Modern Motor Truck,* published in 1921, contains many illustrations of dump bodies. He describes coal bodies with a fixed hopper that fed out into chutes the height of workers' shoulders. He also mentions an early dumping "combination" body that could be used as a flatbed or stake body. The tailgate was hinged at the bottom so the body could be flat. However the tailgate also served as the frame for a slightly smaller gate, hinged at the top. The smaller gate's position could be controlled from inside the cab, allowing the rig to be used for spreading purposes.

Page also describes the functioning of the various styles of hoists. For example, the main portion of a Wood vertical hoist "is a hydraulic cylinder in which a piston moves, the construction being very similar to that of a plunger elevator. The surface of the piston rests on a quantity of oil which is pumped under it by means

Acason trucks were built in Detroit from 1915 until 1925. This circa 1920 tractor has a Fruehauf semitrailer that dumps. It's lifted by the vertical hydraulic hoists in the front. *Fruehauf*

of a rotary gear pump. By having the entire cylinder barrel filled with oil, it will be evident that if a valve is turned so the pump takes the oil from the top of the piston and directs it to the space below the piston, that the member will be raised. A reverse action will cause the piston to descend in the cylinder. The rotary gear

Loading an early 1920s Autocar at an excavation site. The photo was originally distributed by Caterpillar. *Baker Library, Harvard University*

Chicago trucks were assembled in Chicago from 1919 through 1932. This early 1920s model, operated by the City of Joliet, Illinois, has a Heil body. *The Heil Co.*

pump… is driven by a chain and sprocket mechanism from some part of the power transmission system."

Many motor truck manufacturers published "trade" booklets showing how their trucks were employed in specific uses. In the early 1920s, Mack Trucks issued a 25-page booklet entitled *Earth Moving and Hauling of Building and Road Materials*. The introduction states:

> It does not take long to find the weak spots in a motor truck when it is applied to hauling earth and materials for building and road construction. So exacting are the conditions under which a truck normally operates in this field, that the work may be truthfully called the hardest service a motor truck is called upon to render.

The Mack booklet used a whole page to explain why chain and sprocket drive was superior to drive shafts for dump truck applications. The overall weight of the truck was less and road clearance was higher. When the difficulties of a truck's assignment changed, say, from hauling in and out of gravel pits to operating on smooth roads, the sprocket could be changed to better fit the power train to its needs. Lastly, wear and tear and strain on the entire system usually resulted first in a broken chain link, which the driver could repair using common hand tools. The booklet includes many photos of trucks in action at excavations and road building sites, and explains the features of several dump bodies offered.

Reo Motor Car Company offered medium-sized trucks on its Reo Speed Wagon chassis. The company stressed in its brochure that its truck chassis were better adapted to many markets than were larger chassis:

> Contractors, road builders, gravel haulers, and coal and coke dealers are among the many extensive users of Speed Wagons equipped with dump bodies, and who have found Speed Wagon fleetness and operating economy more than offset the extra carrying capacity of the larger, costlier vehicles. The ills suffered by the retail coal trade more than any other is the high cost of delivering 1-ton lots in 3-ton trucks.
> For road building… delivery from the central mixing plant in smaller lots keeps the workmen uniformly busy instead of standing around between big loads.

The booklet also said that hand-powered hoists were the most commonly specified for the Reo-mounted dump bodies.

Most of the dump trucks pictured in this book are on large chassis. Given the nature of their work, that's not surprising. Lighter trucks far outnumbered the big ones, although it is not known how many of the light trucks had dump bodies. On December 31, 1921, according to Harlan Appelquist, slightly more than half of the 1.3 million trucks in the United States were Fords. The next 10 together accounted for 23 percent of the market. They were, in descending order, Republic, Reo, Dodge Brothers, White, International, Chevrolet, GMC, Autocar, Maxwell, and Overland. Note that most of them were firms that built small or, at least, all sizes of trucks; only Autocar was not in the small truck market.

So large was the number of Fords that some body builders covered that market only. For example, the United Automotive Body Co. of Cleveland published a 30-page booklet with commercial bodies for Ford T and TT chassis. The gravity dump body had exterior metal rails on each side. At the bottom front and rear corners of the body were spooled wheels that ran along the rails. When dumping, the rear rail wheel would go down to the track and would reach the bottom of the "U" shape when the body was tilted at the greatest angle. When the body was raised, the front rail wheel would go down a gentler slope and reach its bottom when the body was level. The elaborate system apparently made for a more cushioned operation than merely letting the body drop.

Two other builders of bodies for Fords were the Woonsocket firm and the Griscom-Russell Company. In 1926, Woonsocket advertised dump and elevating coal bodies for both Fords and Chevrolets. Griscom-Russell was apparently the manufacturer of the "Jiffy" dump express body. Both makes appear in the 1926 catalog of the Interboro Hoist and Body Corporation of Long Island City. Another brand of hoist and body mentioned in the catalog was "Auglaize," but the manufacturer was unspecified (an Auglaize truck had been built in New Bremen, Ohio, between 1911 and 1916, and this could have been a related or successor company).

Cook trucks were built in Kankakee, Illinois, in the early 1920s. *Kankakee County Historical Society*

This is a Diamond-T truck, built in Chicago. The vertical hoist behind the cab is PTO driven. *Press Tank & Equipment Co., Chicago*

An early 1920s FWD with right-hand steering and a Heil body. Its owner was the Minnesota Highway Department. *The Heil Co.*

The majority of the Interboro catalog's pages were devoted to well-known makes: Galion, Wood, and St. Paul.

A 1922 price list from the Detroit Trailer Company listed 22 different side dump bodies, with the main difference being capacity. Five of the models had dual hoppers. All were "gravity" dumps, meaning that ideally they could be dumped with little effort after being unlatched. The firm sold three types of two-wheel trailers that dumped to the rear, using a hand hoist, as well as horse-drawn four-wheel garbage dump trailers.

Twin City Motor Truck literature from the early 1920s shows that the Minneapolis-based firm built and

Packard built motor trucks until the mid-1920s. This is a short-wheelbase 1920 Packard used for carrying freshly mixed concrete and dumping it. There are two 1-yard gravity dump hoppers. On each side of the hopper are rails that confine the hopper's downward path, keeping it from moving from side to side. At the front of the hopper is the lock and release mechanism.

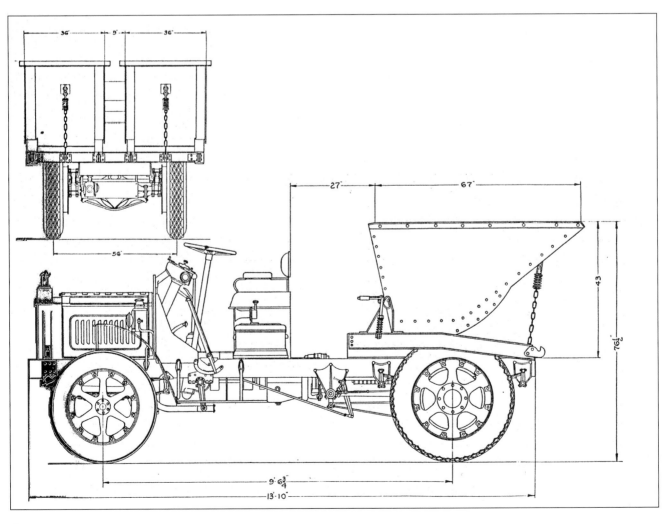

sold dump bodies along with its trucks. Twin City's regular 3-1/2-ton trucks had a 168-inch wheelbase, while its dump trucks used a shorter wheelbase, 156 inches. The shorter wheelbase reflects the fact that dump trucks carried heavier loads and needed a shorter turning radius. The dump body was lifted by a Wood hydraulic hoist operated by the driver in his seat.

Pierce-Arrow truck literature from 1924 lists 10 dump bodies, although the body manufacturer was not specified. The bodies fit three sizes of Pierce-Arrow chassis. Some were made of steel and others were steel-lined wooden bodies. Capacity ranged from 3 to 5 yards. Borg & Beck built the hoists, which were mounted below the chassis. The literature contains a testimonial written in 1923 from the owner of a San Francisco "auto and team" hauling company that praised the performance of his 1911 Pierce-Arrow, which he had named "Betsy":

Consider the work of a dirt truck job compared to the usual commercial truck. It takes two minutes to load a dirt truck from a Steam Shovel. This shovel drops big rocks and big loads of dirt all in a hunk. Then the truck goes to a soft dirt dump where the hind wheels go down in this dump 1 to 2 feet. This means a severe strain to get away from the dump, and most of our hauling is short work, say 20 to 100 loads a day, and average 6 to 7 tons to a load. Now a commercial truck takes a half-hour to unload, a half-hour to load, works on good streets, and makes maybe 5 or 6 loads a day. Just think what Betsy has done; run about 200,000 miles and hauled about 1,000,000 tons of material and still going.

A price list from the mid-1920s for Mack Steel Dump Bodies contains illustrations of bodies on both AB and AC (Bulldog) models. The list proclaims, "the present line of Mack dump bodies is the result of experience that dates back to the old original Mack chain hoist, which was one of the first dumping devices used on a motor truck." Trucks in the illustrations have solid rubber tires. The dump bodies were made with 27

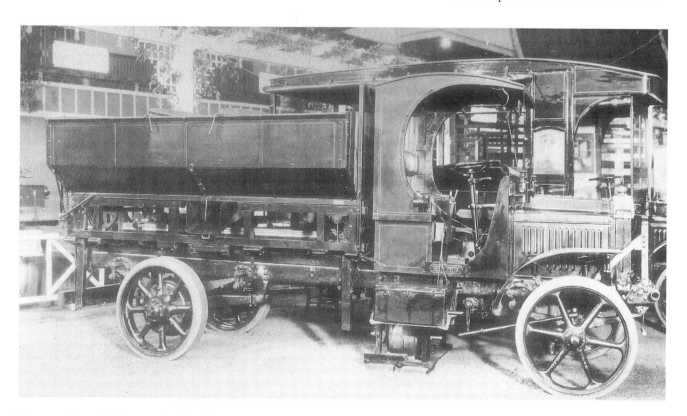

The truck is a Selden, and a handwritten note on the rear of the photo says that it was taken at a 1921 truck show. The Selden firm was founded by the man who was best known for his "automobile" patent that Henry Ford successfully fought. The truck has an elevating coal body with all four corners being lifted simultaneously. There appears to be an electric motor below the cab and an electric cord leading upward. Our guess is that the body was usually lifted by the truck's PTO but, since the truck is inside an exhibition hall, the electric motor has been substituted to demonstrate the raising and lowering of the body. In the middle of the body is a small chute. *American Automobile Manufacturers Assn.*

gauge (3/16-inch) steel plate. Headboards, 6 inches higher than the sides, came with all but the largest bodies. Most bodies had slots so that planks could be added as additional sideboards. (Planks were often used for sideboards, because when trucks were loaded with steam shovels, the shovel's bucket would sometimes hit

Service trucks were produced in Wabash, Indiana, from 1911 through 1933. A Heil hydraulically hoisted dump body was placed on this early 1920s Service chassis for use by the Wabash County Highway Department. *The Heil Co.*

and damage the sideboard. It was easier to replace the planks from time to time than to take dents out of a thick metal sideboard.) Tailgates were also usually higher than the sides and hinged at the top. At the bottom of each dump body, on the right and left sides were "running boards," which were extensions of the bottom plate accommodating vertical side braces on the body's outside. A number of "extras" could also be purchased, including sideboards; partitions that swung from the top and could be locked in place or released with a manual lever; coal chutes, usually part of the tailgate, which allowed small quantities of coal to be released; and spreader chains, which allowed the tailgate to open at the bottom by only 2 or 3 inches and were used to spread materials at an even flow.

Chassis extras included additional "helper" springs that supplemented the truck's standard springs.

Three makes of bodies were offered with the Macks: Wood (a predecessor of Gar Wood), Heil, and St. Paul. Wood bodies with PTO-powered vertical hydraulic hoists ranged from 2- to 10-yard capacity, with the 2-, 2-1/2- and 3-yard bodies intended for AB Macks and the 4-, 5-, 6-, 7-, 8-, 9-, and 10-yard bodies for the AC Macks. Prices ranged from $725 to $1,025. A variation on the 4- to 10-yard bodies was the "slant" hoist, on which the piston behind the cab was slanted slightly, about 10 degrees, toward the rear. There was no price difference between the vertical and slanted hoist installations. Also offered were PTO-powered Wood underbody hoists. They were priced slightly

This early 1920s White has an elaborate special body for placing a load of bricks onto the ground. *Volvo/White*

higher, about $30 to $40. Heil bodies with underbody hydraulic hoists were offered at the same price as the Wood units. St. Paul underbody hydraulic hoists were offered at prices that were about $25 higher per unit than the other two makes.

Springfield body literature shows a 1-cubic-yard gravity dump body intended for Chevrolet chassis. It was a gravity dump body with the fulcrum behind the rear axle and about 1 foot ahead of the rear of the frame. The body was 90 inches long, 49-1/2 inches wide at the front, and 52-1/2 inches wide at the rear. Springfield also offered a flatbed body that could be dumped by using a hand-cranked hoist. This was intended for carriers of general freight who occasionally might want the dumping feature.

Hand hoists operated in a variety of ways. Some were long, continuous screws; others were series of gear wheels. Literature from the Rock Manufacturing Company of Waterloo, New York, describes how a hand-powered scissors-lift worked: The lifting mechanism "consists, essentially, of upper and lower pairs of lifting arms, the forward ends of which are attached to the body and chassis. These arms are hinged together to form a toggle. Between the pairs of arms, at the front end, is interposed a shaft, carrying rollers, which is forced back between the arms by the action of the winch. This separates the arms something after the manner in which the blades of a pair of shears are opened by sliding a pencil between them." Pictures in the literature show bodies mounted on a Ford AA. Operators needed to put some thought into how far back on the truck frame to place the hoisting mechanism, since the closer it was to the body hinge at the rear, the steeper would be the angle of lift.

Martin-Parry, a well-known builder of bodies for light trucks, published a booklet showing truck bodies it would place on 1926 Chevrolet chassis. Martin-Parry offered an all-steel gravity dump body with a patented Sureshot arm that absorbed the shock of the sudden dump and also held the dumped body in position, rather than having it slam back into level position once the box was emptied. The second body was equipped with a hand hoist, requiring 3-1/2 turns to elevate the body; it could be held at any level so it could be used in spreading operations. Martin-Parry also offered a 2-ton soft coal dump body with a chute opening in the center of the tailgate. The truck buyer also had to choose from four cab styles, including one that was an open seat.

The Heil dump body on this Harvey truck is lifted hydraulically with two pistons. Harvey trucks were built in Harvey, Illinois (in the Chicago area), from 1911 until 1922. *The Heil Co.*

In 1928 Martin-Parry published a sales manual for both its own staff and for light truck dealers. It noted that when one buys a truck he or she often must buy the body separately. Usually the truck chassis dealer also had brochures from body builders and sold both the chassis and the body. The chassis was either delivered to the truck dealer or the body builder to have the body installed. There were no firm rules as to who did what, and some chassis builders aligned themselves with body builders and advertised and sold complete units. The Martin-Parry sales manual

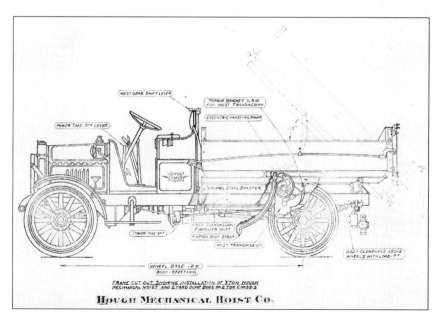

Drawing of a PTO-driven mechanical hoist dated 1921. *Auto Truck*

Kalamazoo trucks were built in Kalamazoo for about 10 years, starting in 1913. This circa 1922 model was purchased by the City of Oshkosh, Wisconsin, and was outfitted with a mechanically operated Highway hoist and 2-cubic-yard dump body. *Dorsey Trailers, Edgerton, Wisconsin*

This is an early 1920s Winther, used by a Kenosha, Wisconsin, sewer contractor. It was equipped with a Highway mechanical hoist. *Dorsey Trailers, Edgerton, Wisconsin*

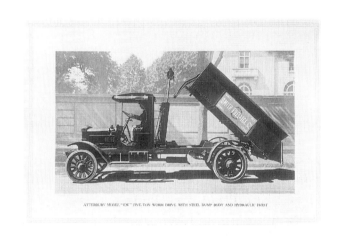

This is an early 1920s Atterbury, built in Buffalo. The vertical hydraulic hoist is visible. The operator was a fuel and ice company, whose combination of products allowed the firm to stay busy in both winter and summer. *William F. Harrah Automobile Foundation*

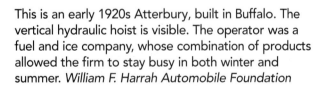

This picture was in a brochure for the Mandt Automatic Dump Body, a gravity dump body shown on a Ford TT chassis. *Lorin Sorensen*

A circa 1921 Wilson, built in Detroit, with a hydraulic Heil body. *The Heil Co.*

An Oshkosh Express chassis from the 1920s, used by a coal company. The Express chassis had rear-wheel drive; most Oshkosh trucks had all-wheel drive. *Oshkosh Truck Corporation*

A Harvey tractor with a Trailmobile trailer and a hoist and dump body, circa 1922. *Pullman Trailmobile*

An early 1920s Packard with a Press dump body, lifted by twin vertical hoists. The cab has snap-on side curtains and a rolled-up door. Note that the center of the dump body is ahead of the rear axle. Packard engineering bulletins of this era recommended that the load's center of gravity should be such that 10 to 15 percent rested on the truck's front axle. *Press Tank & Equipment Co., Chicago*

covered 50 vocations. Here's the start of its suggested sales talk to a road builder:

Mr. Roadbuilder, you realize the importance of speed in your work. In fact your very success in a large measure depends upon it.

First you want the body that will stand the gaff day in and day out of getting materials to where the work is being done and hauling away the materials taken from the excavation. Then it would be a big advantage to you to have a body that would do batch work without having to change equipment. For excavation, speed is required. It's just a matter of mathematics that the faster you remove a given quantity of dirt, the faster you haul it away, dump it, and get back to the job, the more the costs of doing the work are reduced. This means bigger profits and that job is exactly the kind of job this gravity dump body will do.

A 1922 ad for Van Dorn dump bodies and hoist. The truck is an early 1920s Packard. *American Automobile Manufacturers Assn.*

The salesperson was also to look at the sales talk for excavators, which contained more details about the body's quality, and operation of the dumping mechanism. The salesperson was told to close by discussing "comfort to drivers, service, and guarantee features."

Other dump body literature of this era also emphasized the importance of speed. A Heil brochure said: "The Heil Hoist is at least 1/4 to 1/2 of a minute faster at the same engine speed. Twenty trucks hauling twenty loads each day save 3 hours and twenty minutes, or about $15.00, more than enough to pay the wages of two good drivers."

An article in the April 1930 issue of *The Commercial Car Journal* listed 27 manufacturers of dump bodies. They were: Anthony Co., Streator, Illinois; Auto Truck Equipment Co., Pittsburgh; Auto Truck Steel Body Co., Chicago; Best Body Co., Coatsville, Pennsylvania; Commercial Shearing & Stamping Co., Youngstown, Ohio; Easton Car & Construction Co., Easton, Pennsylvania; Differential Steel Car Co., Findlay, Ohio; Galion Allsteel Body Co., Galion, Ohio; Fitz Gibbon & Crisp, Trenton, New Jersey; Hercules Products, Inc., Evansville, Indiana; Heil Co., Milwaukee; Highway Trailer Co., Edgerton, Wisconsin; Hockensmith Wheel & Mine Car Co., Penn, Pennsylvania; Hughes-Keenan Co., Mansfield, Ohio; Jorgenson Dump Body Co., Milwaukee; Lee Trailer & Body Co., Plymouth, Indiana; Marion Steel Body Co., Marion, Ohio; Mayer Body Corp., Pittsburgh; Martin-Parry Corp., York, Pennsylvania; McNamara Bros., Baltimore; Moore Body Co., Reading, Pennsylvania; New

American-LaFrance was the nation's premier builder of fire apparatus for much of the twentieth century; its name now belongs to Freightliner. In the 1920s, American-LaFrance also built commercial chassis for other tasks. This photo, taken in 1923, shows a Heil dump body powered by a hydraulic hoist. *The Heil Co.*

York Central Iron Works, Hagerstown, Maryland; Rodenhausen Wagon Works, Philadelphia; St. Paul Hydraulic Hoist Co., St. Paul; Superior Body Co., Marion, Indiana; Waterloo Bodies, Inc., Waterloo, New York; and Wood Hydraulic Hoist & Body Co., Detroit. Many trucks with dump bodies were pictured in this 1930 article. Only one had the vertical hydraulic hoists; all other installations were underbody hoists.

An accompanying article in the same issue listed builders of mechanical and hydraulic hoists used for dump bodies. Hoist manufacturers, in addition to many of the firms listed in the previous paragraph, included: Detroit Trailer & Machine, Detroit; Eagle Wagon Co., Auburn, New York; Marquette Mfg. Co., St. Paul; Moore Body Co., Reading; National Steel Products Co., Kansas City, Missouri; Perfection Steel Body Co., Galion, Ohio; Rock Mfg. Co., Waterloo, New York; Simplex Body & Mfg. Co., Conneautville, Pennsylvania; Steinke Bros. Mfg. Co., Peoria; Universal Hoist & Body Co., Everett, Massachusetts; Utility Trailer Mfg. Co., Los Angeles; Van Dorn Iron Works Co., Cleveland; and Warner Elevator Mfg. Co. of Cincinnati. Hoists would be sold to numerous truck body builders who would install them under bodies they were fitting to individual customers' truck chassis.

Still another article in the same issue dealt with six-wheel attachments, which added an additional weight-bearing axle to the rear of the powered axle. This increased the truck's carrying capacity in both physical and legal terms. The new axle had to be attached to the frame, and adjustments were usually needed in the truck's rear suspension so the load would be shared by both rear axles. In all of the 10 versions discussed, the new axle was "dead" in the sense that it transmitted neither power nor braking. Later versions would link the two rear axles with heavy-duty bicycle-like chains between the wheels of both axles.

Some literature published in 1928 by the Commercial Shearing & Stamping Company described its "three-way" hoist and dump body, available in capacities ranging from 1-1/2 to 15 tons. The body's tailgate and sideboards were all hinged at the bottom. The truck would be loaded with sideboards and tailgate locked. Upon arriving at the dump site, the driver—using controls inside the cab—would lock the body to the frame along the side toward which the load was to be dumped. He would activate the underbody hydraulic hoist, which would lift the body, dumping toward the side whose bottom was locked to the truck frame. The sideboard (or tailgate) on the dumping side would be unlocked and drop fully open by the time the body was at a 16-degree angle. When dumping toward the rear, the dumping angle could be as high as 70 degrees; to either side it could be as high as 54 degrees. The company's literature suggests these applications in which the three-way dump feature would be useful:

> *Road work: berming, shoulders, backfilling behind curbs, hauling road mesh, hauling rooted stumps, and spreading.*
> *Building construction: hand loading of sand, gravel, etc., dumping at curb without blocking city street.*
> *Coal dealers: chutes load through coal door directly into sidewalk coal hole—from either side without blocking traffic.*

An early 1920s Autocar with a trailer for unloading bricks. *Pullman Trailmobile*

It appears that the container holding the bricks travels backward a short distance as the platform is lifted. *Pullman Trailmobile*

The literature also said that the three-way dump bodies were better investments for trucking contractors, as they were more versatile than conventional rear dumps. They could do anything that a rear-dump truck could, and often the trucking contractor could charge a premium for use of the side dump feature. One brochure contained pictures of three-way dump bodies on a variety of chassis: Brockway, Diamond-T, Indiana, International, Linn, Mack, Pierce-Arrow, Stewart, Ward-LaFrance, and White.

Ford distributed TRUCKFAX sheets to its dealers, whose salesmen were to keep them in loose-leaf binders. A compilation of sheets, from about 1930, included about 20 pages dealing with dump bodies and hoists. There was the Bruder three-way dump body; a high-lift coal body built by Palm Body Company of Reading; coal bodies built by Edwards Iron Works of South Bend; plus bodies built by Anthony, Best, Eagle, Galion, Hughes-Keenan, Lee, Marion, St. Paul, and Wood. An interesting adaptation was called the "Flexadrive," built by the Western Manufacturing Company of Detroit. It eliminated the Ford AA's cab and added a rearward facing driver's seat (above the fender on the driver's side) plus steering wheel and foot controls, all facing the rear of the truck. The dump body was conventionally mounted, although it could be longer since the truck had no cab. The truck then was steered from the rear with power at the front, and was intended for use in situations with short, repetitive dump movements.

Late in the 1920s some manufacturers experimented with aluminum truck bodies, including dump bodies. The G. A. Fuller Coal Company of St. Louis replaced a 1,600-pound steel body with a 600-pound aluminum body, increasing the payload by 1,000 pounds. Fuller translated this to an annual savings of $1,200.

During the 1920s states began regulating the size and weights of trucks. Each state's formula was different, and many of the details dealt with the weight on each

A Perfection body on a 1923–1924 Chevrolet. The body was raised by hand crank, with its handle visible by the rear tire. *Perfection Cobey*

axle and the distance between axles. Since dump trucks often operated with heavy loads, they were especially affected by weight restrictions. These regulations had considerable impact on the design of dump bodies and their placement on truck chassis. In a technological sense, the dump body and hoist that we know today are not very different from the ones we would have seen in 1930.

Page from a brochure for Easton Scoop Bodies, built for Ford TT trucks. *Lorin Sorensen*

A Mandt gravity dump body on a 1920s Ford TT. Dotted lines show how three cover doors would open. *Reliance*

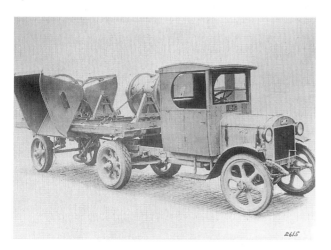

A 1923 GMC with a trailer body consisting of several side-dumping units. The units are locked in place and, when unlocked, dump by gravity's forces. *L. E. Reznicek*

This truck is a Kenworth from 1923, the first year that the Kenworth name appeared. The hoist, chain driven off the truck's PTO, was built by the Young Iron Works of Seattle. *Kenworth Truck Co.*

Rear view of a Mack Bulldog with no cab roof. Many dump trucks of this era had no cabs because construction work was carried on only during good weather. *Mack Museum*

The body is hoisted by a continuous screw. Note the tire chains. *Mack Museum*

An early 1920s Moreland with twin rear axles, being loaded by a steam shovel. *Bill West*

Above: Titan trucks were built in Milwaukee from 1917 until the late 1920s. This one, sold to a user in Madison, Wisconsin, has a Heil body with what appears to be a mechanical lift. *The Heil Co.*

Above: Chicago was the home for Old Reliable trucks, built from 1911 until 1927. This one, used by a coal company, has a Heil twin-piston hydraulic hoist. *The Heil Co.*

A Highway hoist and dump body on a circa 1923 Oshkosh. *Dorsey Trailers, Edgerton, Wisconsin*

An early 1920s Packard used in a road paving project in California. Note the steamroller in the background. *CALTRANS Photo Archives*

Illustrating
No. 1105
with No. 431
"Serv-All" Cab

An excerpt from a Martin-Parry catalog shows a hand-hoist dump body for a 1924 Chevrolet. *The William F. Harrah Automobile Foundation*

Delivering coal in Cleveland with a 1924 White. The truck has acetylene lamps and no cab. *Volvo/White*

DeMartini trucks were built in San Francisco from 1918 until 1934, after which the firm continued building trash-collection bodies. This DeMartini is from the early 1920s, and has a dump body. *George DeMartini*

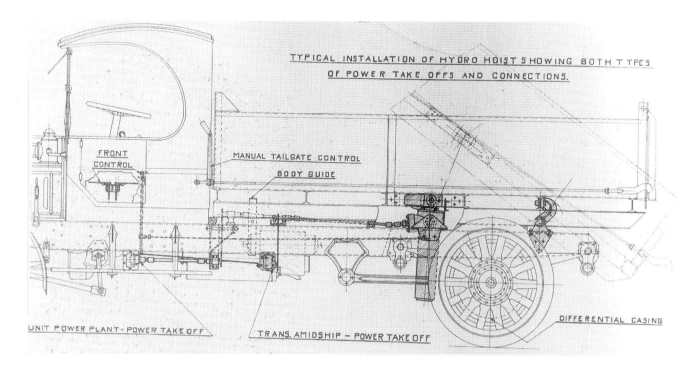

TYPICAL INSTALLATION OF HYDRO HOIST SHOWING BOTH TYPES
OF POWER TAKE OFFS AND CONNECTIONS.

FRONT
CONTROL

MANUAL TAILGATE CONTROL

BODY GUIDE

DIFFERENTIAL CASING

UNIT POWER PLANT - POWER TAKE OFF

TRANS. AMIDSHIP - POWER TAKE OFF

This drawing is from a mid-1920s manual containing instructions for installing Heil dump bodies. *Chuck Rhoads*

A 1924 White making a coal delivery in Milwaukee. Note the empty coal basket on the truck's roof. *Volvo/White*

Armleder trucks were built in Cincinnati. This tractor, from the 1920s, pulls a trailer with a mechanical hoist consisting of many gear wheels. *National Automotive History Collection, Detroit Public Library*

Gotfredson trucks were built in Detroit, and this one, from the mid-1920s, has a Heil dump body. *The Heil Co.*

A mid-1920s International being loaded by a steam shovel. *Navistar Archives*

This is not a dump truck, but note how the load is being dumped. A mid-1920s International with a straight grain body is shown being lifted in the front at a Canadian grain elevator. *National Archives of Canada*

Trade magazine ad for a Tusco hoist, shown on a mid-1920s International. *Pullman Trailmobile*

TUSCO Double Duty Truck Hoist
For Dumping   and Loading

This hoist will solve your trucking problems economically. Hoist mounted below truck body, entirely out of way. For loading tractors, implements, etc. Will dump load any desired angle. Make your truck earn more, save 75% on delivery cost.

ARNO SCHMECHEL & SON, INC.   **Thiensville, Wis.**

This is a mid-1920s Kelly, built in Springfield, Ohio. It has a Heil hydraulic-lift body and a grille guard. *The Heil Co.*

This is a LeMoon truck, from the 1920s, with a dump body. LeMoons were built in Chicago from 1910 until 1939. *Press Tank & Equipment Co., Chicago*

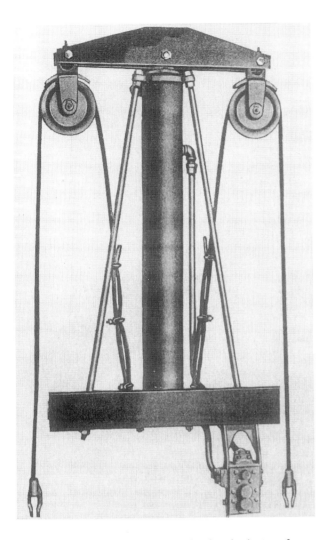

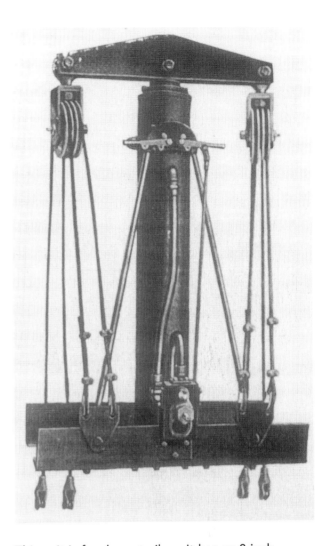

Here are two St. Paul vertical hydraulic hoists from the mid-1920s. This one is for truck bodies. The cylinder is 6 inches in diameter and takes up 7-3/4 inches behind the cab. *Chuck Rhoads*

This unit is for dump trailers. It has an 8-inch diameter and double pulleys. *Chuck Rhoads*

This is a Rock Hand Hoist, built in Waterloo, New York. The crank is on the lower right and as it winds the cable, it opens the jaws in the center, raising the body.

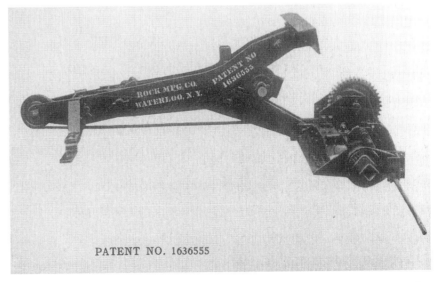

PATENT NO. 1636555

Bodies and Hoists for **IHC**
by (PENN)

PENN BODY DIVISION

(PENN)
TRUCK BODIES

THE HOCKENSMITH CORPORATION

PENN, PENNSYLVANIA

TELEPHONE
LAFAYETTE
3-5401

This is the original artwork for the cover of a Penn Body brochure in the mid-1920s intended for distribution to International truck dealers. Brochures like this would have the cover tailored to each make of truck, but the inside photos would show bodies only and no specific truck makes could be identified. *Hockensmith Corp.*

Here are some Ruggles trucks that have been equipped with Highway mechanical hoists and 2-cubic-yard dump bodies. Ruggles trucks were built in Saginaw during the 1920s. *Dorsey Trailers, Edgerton, Wisconsin*

An elevated Heil coal body that feeds out from the bottom, mounted on a circa 1926 Federal chassis. *The Heil Co.*

A 1926 GMC "Big Brute" with twin rear axles. The rear wheels are of different size. *Bill West*

A coal body on a 1926 Chevrolet chassis, with a bulkhead allowing the truck to carry two separate orders. The release-lever for the bulkhead is visible to the right. *National Automotive History Collection, Detroit Public Library*

Double acting tailgate man

This is an Auglaize hand hoist from the mid-1920s. It was intended for lighter loads. *Chuck Rhoads*

This is a mid-1920s Graham Bros. truck with a Heil dump body. At this time Graham Bros. shared chassis and metalwork with Dodge autos. *The Heil Co.*

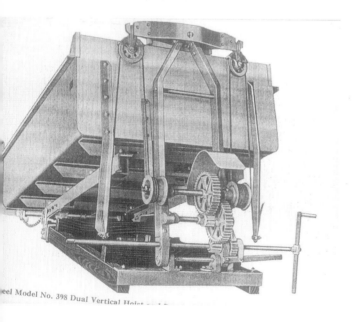

eel Model No. 398 Dual Vertical Hoist

This is a Galion hand hoist sold in the mid-1920s. *Chuck Rhoads*

This is a Hurlbut truck with a dump body lifted by a vertical hoist. Hurlbut trucks were built in New York City from 1912 until 1927. *Frank Malatesta*

A 1926 Hug with a ready-mix body for carrying wet concrete short distances. Hug trucks were built in Highland, Illinois, from 1922 until 1942. *Chuck Rhoads*

A 1926 Stoughton with a dump body on display at the Hays Antique Truck Museum in Woodland, California. Stoughton trucks were built in Stoughton, Wisconsin, between 1920 and 1928.

A 1926 Moreland with twin side-dump bodies used in a copper mining operation in Jerome, Arizona. *Bill West*

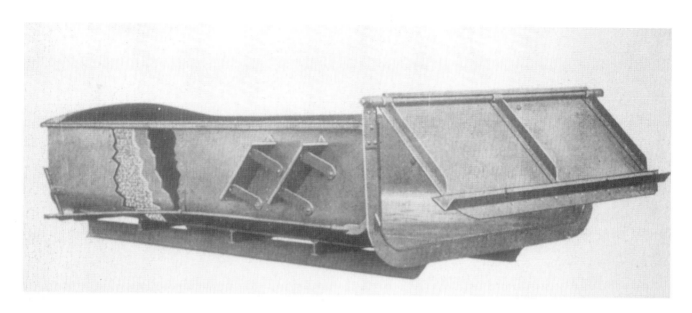

This is a Heil insulated asphalt body from the late 1920s. A 3/8-inch layer of asbestos was placed between the body shells to help keep the load warm until it was dumped. Note the two steps (that are parallel to the ground when the body is in dumping position); they are for workers to stand on while cleaning out the load. *Chuck Rhoads*

A mid-1920s White dump truck with a Christie Crawler conversion, consisting of a second axle and tread encircling tires of both axles. Coil springs keep tension on the track. *Harry J. Mann*

Two views of a dump truck, probably a Diamond-T, backing up a long trestle to dump its load into a barge. It is possible the trestle is high because of fluctuations in water levels. *Reliance*

A Ford TT with a wet concrete-hauling body dumping into a device that is used for paving.
Portland Cement Association

This body was made for heavy-duty work. It has a large winch behind the cab, a hoist on a derrick that has ground support, and a dump body. *Auto Truck*

"DITWILER"

The only self locking Hand Hoist dump body on the market.

Locks itself in its own worm and worm wheel mechanism.

Ditwiler Model G-1 Dump Body Mounted on Graham G-Boy Chassis

Graham Bros. Chassis	Ditwiler SAFTEE Hand Hoist Dump Body	Capacity	Size	List Price
Model BC	Model G-1	1 cu. yd	90x52x10	$155.00
Extension Sides to Increase capacity of Model G-1 to 1½ cu. yd.			- - - - - -	15.00
Model CC or MC	Model G-2	1½ cu. yd.	96x60x12	$190.00
Extension Sides to increase capacity of Model G-2 to 2 cu. yd.			- - - - -	15.00
Model OC or OCR	Model G-3	2 cu. yd.	96x60x16	$225.00
Extension Sides to Increase capacity of Model G-3 to 2¾ cu. yd.			- - - - -	15.00
	The Above Model Can be Furnished in Removable Side Type for $20.00 Additional			
Model GG4	Garbage or Rubbish Body	2 cu. yd.	108x60x18	$225.00

This is one side of an advertising card distributed by Ditwiler Manufacturing Company showing how four sizes of its hand-hoist bodies could be fitted to three different 1927 Graham Bros. truck chassis. A hoist crank is visible at the lower front of the dump body. The Ditwiler firm was a predecessor to Hercules Galion Products, Inc. *Peabody-Galion*

The Hughes-Keenan Company of Mansfield, Ohio, built this underbody hand hoist for Chevrolet and Graham Bros. chassis. We are looking at it from the top. A hand crank fits at the upper left, and we can see several sets of gear wheel reductions that transform the human's strength into lifting capability. *John Steighner*

These two photos are from an original sheet from a Hockensmith truck body salesman's catalog. This is a manually operated dump body on a 1927–1928 Chevrolet chassis. *Hockensmith Corp.*

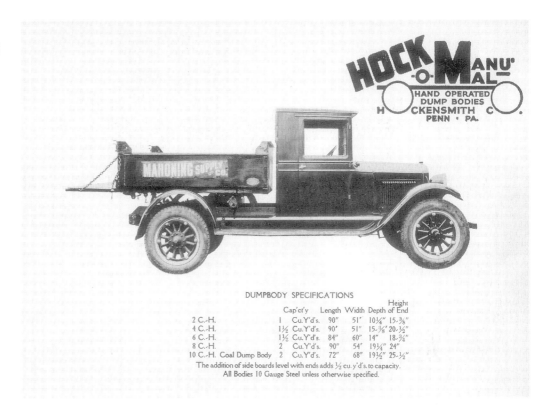

DUMPBODY SPECIFICATIONS

	Cap'ct'y	Length	Width	Height Depth of End
2 C.-H.	1 Cu.Y'd's.	90"	51"	10¼" 15-⅜"
4 C.-H.	1½ Cu.Y'd's.	90"	51"	15-⅜" 20-½"
6 C.-H.	1½ Cu.Y'd's.	84"	60"	14" 18-¾"
8 C.-H.	2 Cu.Y'd's.	90"	54"	19¼" 24"
10 C.-H. Coal Dump Body	2 Cu.Y'd's.	72"	68"	19½" 25-½"

The addition of side boards level with ends adds ½ cu. y'd's. to capacity.
All Bodies 10 Gauge Steel unless otherwise specified.

This sheet shows a garbage body, enclosed at the bottom and with covers for the top of the load. *Hockensmith Corp.*

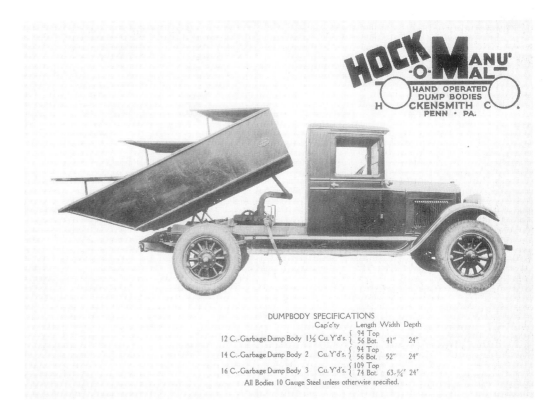

DUMPBODY SPECIFICATIONS

	Cap'c'ty	Length	Width	Depth
12 C.-Garbage Dump Body	1½ Cu. Y'd's.	94 Top / 56 Bot.	41"	24"
14 C.-Garbage Dump Body	2 Cu. Y'd's.	94 Top / 56 Bot.	52"	24"
16 C.-Garbage Dump Body	3 Cu. Y'd's.	109 Top / 74 Bot.	63-¾"	24"

All Bodies 10 Gauge Steel unless otherwise specified.

This is a circa 1928 Selden Roadmaster with a dump body. *American Automobile Manufacturers Assn.*

A 1928 Mack with a Mack-built hoist and dump body. It was exported to Argentina. *Jorge A. Matiré*

PENN *Automatic* DUMP BODIES
(PATENTED)
for FORD TRUCKS

1929

Body in Place on Ford Truck

Outstanding ADVANTAGES

PENN Dump Bodies are made by an established, reputable company which has been manufacturing transportation equipment for 50 years. The plant located at Penn, Pa., in the heart of the Pittsburgh district, is in close proximity to the steel producing companies. The factory is equipped with the latest and finest machinery for shearing, fabricating, riveting, and welding, combined with ample foundry facilities. Penn bodies are made in the plant—not just assembled—which permits complete production control. Only the finest obtainable materials are used. Continuous and rigid inspection is maintained. Service and satisfaction are assured, for the company stands back of its products!

HOCKENSMITH CO . . . PENN, PA.

This ad, run by the Hockensmith Company in 1929, shows a gravity dump body on a Ford AA. *Hockensmith Corp.*

This is the view looking down into a 1928 Hug with a compartmentalized body that allowed "blending" several different grades of materials as they were dumped. *Chuck Rhoads*

A 1929 Chevrolet with a dump body installed by McCabe-Powers of St. Louis. *McCabe-Powers Body Co.*

A Ford AA with a Heil body raised mechanically by using the hand crank. On this side of the frame is a geared wheel with a pawl that will lock the body in its raised position. When the author was copying these photos some years ago at the Heil offices in Milwaukee, a member of the Heil family chatted with him briefly and said that the hand cranks were considered dangerous because once the body started descending, the crank would revolve furiously and could not be stopped. *The Heil Co.*

This 1929 photo shows a Mack, operated by the Keystone Sand and Gravel Company, outfitted for a parade. On its load of sand has been placed a keystone, shaped out of stones. *Watson & Meehan, San Francisco*

This circa 1930 Fageol has a
Heil hydraulic dump body.
The Heil Co.

The Louisiana Quarry Co. used
this 1929 Hug model 99. The
emblem on side of hood says:
"HUG ROADBUILDER."
Chuck Rhoads

A Hackney gravity dump body on an open 1930 Chevrolet. *Hackney Bros. Body Co.*

A 1930 Indiana dump truck used for carrying sand. The body was built by National Steel Products Co. of Kansas City, Missouri. *Old Cars Weekly*

Stewarts were built from 1912 to 1941 in Buffalo, one of several makes of trucks built in that city. These pictures show a Heil hoist and body on a 1927 Stewart Six. *The Heil Co.*

Two views of a late 1920s Reo with a Heil body. Reos were built in Lansing. *The Heil Co.*

The Heil cement body both
lifts and dumps and is shown
on a 1930 Relay. Relay trucks
were built in Wabash, Indiana,
from 1927 until 1933. The
Relay firm was created by
investors who owned
three other truck makes.
The Heil Co.

A 1930 Mack with twin rear axles and a dump body. Note the horn on the side. *Robert Fulton*

Chapter 4

1931–1940

The Depression and Public Works

This decade is most remembered for the Great Depression. Numerous federal government public works projects provided jobs for the unemployed, and in this way generated demand for dump trucks.

The Baker Equipment Engineering Company, of Richmond, Virginia, produced a 96-page catalog that shows the range of dump bodies offered at this time. It was directed at truck dealers in a four-state area—Virginia, West Virginia, and North and South Carolina. (Baker also had a shop in Charleston, West Virginia.) Baker offered to send its body mounting experts anywhere in the four states to mount the hoists, dump bodies, or other equipment "at the same mounting charges made for the same work at our mounting stations. We pay all expenses, including hotel bill, railroad fare, etc. It is necessary, however, that you supply a shop or garage in which to do the work and render our mechanic the services of one helper. The minimum mounting charge, however, [for which] we would send our mechanic into the territory on this basis is $50."

A 1931 Dodge with a Heil body. Note the spider-shaped radiator protector. *The Heil Co.*

Much of the catalog was devoted to dump hoists and bodies built by the Wood Hydraulic Hoist & Body Co. Wood hoists were described in 5 pages, and Wood dump bodies in 11 pages. Wood gravity dump bodies got a 2-page spread and 1 page each was devoted to garbage, wet mix, and coal bodies. Two pages were devoted to coal bodies built by the Universal Hoist & Body Co. The Differential Steel Car Company's three-way dump bodies also received 2 pages of coverage. Another 2 pages described hand-hoist dump bodies built by the Marion Steel Body Co. Lastly, Galion hand-hoist and gravity dump bodies were described in 2 pages. Chassis to which dump bodies were being fitted usually lacked cabs, so 4 pages of the Baker catalog displayed a variety of cabs, with and without doors.

Catalog prices included the product, freight charges, and installation. A 3-cubic-yard garbage body, made by Wood, cost $289 at the factory. Shipping charges to the Baker shop were $25. Installation cost $25, and the price installed at the Baker shop was $339—the same as if you bought the chassis and shipped it to Baker for body installation. Hoists tended to cost slightly more than the bodies, and the price of cabs (in priming paint), installed, ran between $170 and $400.

A 1931 issue of *American City Magazine* showed photos of the "Von Keller Refuse Collector," which was a large, rotating drum normally sloping downward toward the front of the truck. Garbage was loaded in the rear and the drum rotated continually, causing the debris to move toward the front and be compacted. The article noted, "When used for collecting leaves, it is necessary to start the machine revolving with about 25 gallons of water in the tank, so that the leaves are dampened and easily dumped without blowing about." The body was unloaded by being dumped to the rear, and it could be rotated to keep loads from sticking.

The same publication also had illustrations of other dumping bodies used by municipalities. This included many garbage collection bodies, since nearly all were emptied by dumping. Also included were sanders and spreaders. Some sander and spreader devices were small trailers, carefully attached to the dump truck, which

An early 1930s Fageol tractor pulling two bottom-dump trailers. The rig was operated by a subsidiary of the Southern Pacific Railroad. *Southern Pacific*

were fed through a chute in the truck's tailgate. The spreading device was powered by the device's own wheels (similar to a manual lawn mower). Some spreaders had their own motors and could be more carefully controlled. They were likely used in paving operations.

The workings of a mechanical hoist. Power comes from the PTO on the right. Inside the box, gears slow down and increase the power of thrust and change its direction 90 degrees. Cogs then lift or lower the body. *Auto Truck*

This Heil body on an early 1930s Mack AC opens on the sides to dump. It is possible that it was intended for trash, although some rough notes accompanying the original photo referred to it as a "coal" body. *The Heil Co.*

There were also large spreading units consisting of big steel hoppers that fit inside the lowered dump body.

Many snowplows were pictured, and almost all of them were mounted on the front of trucks with dump bodies. In northern climates, many municipal dump trucks were expected to serve as snowplows in the winter. This placed some additional requirements on the chassis and power plant. These trucks needed stiffer front suspension to absorb the thrust of the plow blade and additional engine cooling capacity because of the low speed and the plow blade blocking the airflow to the radiator. Oversize clutches were also useful. Trucks to be fitted with scraper blades needed sufficient underside space for their placement and operation.

In Wisconsin, where the author grew up, it was common in winter to see city dump trucks either plowing or spreading salted sand. In rural areas, much larger trucks and plows were used. While they were mounted on dump bodies, in some instances the wing blades (farther out than the main V blade) were anchored to braces placed in the dump body. Trucks expected to carry large snowplows in the winter were fitted with a slightly smaller dump body; the increased space between the box and truck cab then housed the masts and hoists, winches, and cable for controlling the snowplow's various blades.

Gar Wood dump body literature from the 1930s indicates that on that firm's bodies, "square bottom corners are standard but round bottom corners are furnished if specified, at no additional cost," and "tapered bodies, with the rear end wider than front end, will be furnished at no extra cost, if specified." Some Gar Wood bodies with twin hydraulic pistons now had the pistons outside the truck's frame, which saved weight.

A 1940 report by the American Public Works Association (APWA) dealt with refuse collection equipment and covered the variety of motorized (and horse-drawn) bodies used. Bodies that emptied to the rear were wider in back to facilitate flow of material. The bodies had to be elevated to at least 45 degrees for ashes and garbage, and 55 degrees for mixed refuse or rubbish. Gravity dump bodies were found mainly on trailers and would dump to either side. Gravity dump bodies that emptied to the rear were unsatisfactory for garbage trucks, because the body's rim was so high, it made the truck difficult for garbage collectors to load from street level. In some cities, sanitation workers used trucks with bodies fixed to the frame, which they would drive to an installation that lifted the whole truck by the front end, allowing the contents to dump.

The APWA report described another system for emptying a truck's load efficiently: "A device that has long been used for rubbish or mixed refuse is called the ladder-chain, which usually consists of two or three

A Stewart tractor with a twin-axle semitrailer and a Heil dumping hoist and body. The truck was used in Solsville, New York. *The Heil Co.*

A pair of circa 1932 Federals used by the Tennessee Valley Authority. *American Automobile Manufacturers Assn.*

This circa 1931 Stewart has a Heil hydraulic dump body and a snowplow mount in front. The wheel we see through the windshield is for adjusting the blade. *The Heil Co.*

chains or cables stretched lengthwise on the floor of the vehicle body with crosswise slats of wood or metal spaced twelve or eighteen inches [apart]. The longitudinal chains or cable are fastened at the back end of the truck, extend along the floor and then up the front end of the body, and terminate at the top in a bridle. Practically the entire contents of a load may be readily stripped from a vehicle by attaching a line from a winch, tractor, or other power mechanism to the bridle and pulling the ladder-chain out the back end of the vehicle. This same device is sometimes powered quite effectively by the vehicle itself, with the bridle attached to a line secured to a suitably placed anchorage or 'dead-man.' "

A 1932 Pierce-Arrow with a large dump body, used by a sand and gravel contractor. It had solid tires in the rear and pneumatic tires in the front. *American Automobile Manufacturers Assn.*

An open-cab 1932 International used to build a road near Naperville, Illinois. *Navistar Archives*

A similar device utilized a template, approximately the shape of a vertical cross-section of the body, placed at the front of the body and attached to several cables leading to the rear. To unload, the operator simply attached the cables to a stationary winch, which pulled the contents from the body.

Dump bottoms were used only on trailers, not trucks, because a truck's driveshaft and axle housings would interfere with the dumping operation. Trailers were usually not used for household collections, but they would be stationed at various locations where trucks that made household collections would dump their garbage. The larger trailers would take the garbage from these transfer stations to the ultimate disposal site.

Nearly all garbage loads on trucks had to be covered. Often the entire body was enclosed and its compartment doors kept shut except during loading. Open trucks needed tarpaulins, or chain or rope netting. Some dump bodies had a steel framework upon which the tarpaulin or netting would be placed; then, as the body filled with garbage, the operator would extend the tarpaulin over the load.

Another issue with garbage bodies was the watertightness of the body. The disadvantage of a conventional dump body was that the liquids would seep out of the rear at the tailgate. Some bodies were designed with no tailgate, and the rear would be sloped so that the rear top would point downward when the body was dumped. In cities where garbage was incinerated, the garbage body sometimes had a perforated subfloor, allowing moisture to drain from the load making it easier to burn. The liquid collected below the subfloor would be drained and dealt with separately.

The APWA report discussed endgate choices as well. The advantage of hinging the endgate at the bottom of the body was that materials would flow out easily when the endgate was opened and the body raised. The disadvantage was that the bottom-hinged endgate was most susceptible to damage as drivers backed up. An endgate hinged at the top was designed to swing freely, but would still impede dumping if it jammed. A third alternative was half-endgates, with each half attached to vertical hinges on each side. At the time of unloading, the operator would unlatch the half-doors, swing them 270 degrees around the side of the truck, where they would be secured, and then dump the load. The article mentions that some cities were experimenting with hydraulically lifted endgates at the time (1940).

Despite the Depression, motor trucks continued to develop and the truck of 1940 could be operated today, although with smaller loads and at slower speeds. Today's heavy-duty trucks, including dump trucks, are usually diesel powered. Diesel power was just being introduced to trucking as the decade of the 1930s ended.

An early 1930s Federal with a hydraulic hoist. In an unusual choice of options, the buyer decided not to buy a cab but did buy chromed louvers. *Auto Truck*

The operator of this 1933–1934 Ford raised his dump body too quickly while delivering a load of driveway gravel in Plymouth, Ohio. *Thomas Root*

A tow truck was summoned to lower the front end gently after the gravel was shoveled out of the rear. *Thomas Root*

James Duclon of Wisconsin, obtained this 1933 Chevrolet from his uncle, who had purchased it in 1945 for use on a farm. The dump body mechanism is off a 1931–1932 Chevrolet parts truck. Here we see it with the body lowered. *James R. Duclon*

Here the body is raised. This is the St. Paul hoist Duclon took off of the parts truck. *James R. Duclon*

Looking down toward the rear we see the drive shaft, a narrower rod that connects the PTO to the hoist, and a cable controlling the hoist. What looks like the top of the chassis frame is a wooden board. *James R. Duclon*

The hydraulic cylinder has pushed the piston straight back in a horizontal direction. *James R. Duclon*

Small rollers ride on tracks parallel to the frame, while larger rollers push on cams that are below the box. *James R. Duclon*

We see large and small rollers, cams, and tracks. *James R. Duclon*

Closer view showing how thrust is transferred. *James R. Duclon*

A 1933 Indiana with dump body, outfitted with all-wheel drive. *Volvo/White*

Two views of an early 1930s FWD with a Heil garbage body used in Yonkers, New York. The duck-tail body is enclosed so that liquid doesn't run out on to the street. *The Heil Co.*

Marmon-Herrington built heavy-duty trucks, starting in the early 1930s. This circa 1933 Marmon-Herrington has a Heil body with a hydraulic lift. *The Heil Co.*

An Oshkosh-powered earthmover from the early 1930s. *Oshkosh Truck Corporation*

Many dump trucks in municipal service also served as snowplows. This picture shows how a Drott snowplow would be attached to an early 1930s Oshkosh chassis with two sets of push bars. *Oshkosh Truck Corporation*

A large White making a coal delivery in downtown Chicago. Commercial buildings often had coal chutes in their sidewalks, covered by iron doors. The man on the right is holding a broom. *Volvo/White*

A 1933–1934 Chevrolet with a Hockensmith dump body. The lever on the corner of the body toward the viewer releases the tailgate. *Hockensmith Corp.*

An Auto Truck dump body on a 1933–1934 Diamond-T chassis. Both the body builder and the chassis builder were located in Chicago. *Auto Truck*

A 1934 Diamond-T with a streamlined dump body. *Auto Truck*

During the 1930s, the Civilian Conservation Corps was a federal program that built public improvements and provided employment for young men. Here, in Rocky Mountain National Park, is a circa 1934 Dodge dump truck with CCC markings and a grille guard. *Rocky Mountain National Park*

Loading a 1933–1935 Dodge with a shovel loader in California. *CALTRANS Photo Archives*

A 3-yard Dominion body with a Commercial hoist on a 1934 FWD chassis. The high headlights are for snowplow duty.

Loading a 1934 International with rock in Grand Canyon. *Grand Canyon National Park*

A 1935 Autocar used by the U.S. Bureau of Public Roads. Headlights on the cowl allow snowplow use. *American Automobile Manufacturers Assn.*

Here's a 1935 Hug Roadbuilder with a Hug-built body. *Chuck Rhoads*

A trio of 1935 Fords dumping into a railroad car. *Free Library of Philadelphia*

A Heil twin-piston body on a 1935 GMC chassis. *The Heil Co.*

Unloading a mid-1930s International at a grain elevator by lifting the front of the entire truck. Grain feeds into a grate on the ground. *Navistar Archives*

85

Linn half-tracks were built in Morris, New York, from 1916 until 1950 and were widely used in logging, mining, and construction. This one is from the 1930s and has a dump body with a cab roof protector. In mining operations Linn eventually lost out to earthmoving machines that ran on large rubber tires at higher speeds.

A 1936 GMC with a dump body and protectors over both hood and head lamps. *American Truck Historical Society*

A streamlined Heil body, probably for home deliveries of coal, on a 1936 Ford chassis. *The Heil Co.*

A mid-1930s Ford dump truck is hoisted up a very steep grade at a dam construction site along the White River in Washington State. To the left we see cables and pulleys, which are connected to a large stationary engine at the top. The truck is pulled up and down the wooden road, carrying loads in either direction. At the far side of the road are rails, used either for wagons with flanged steel wheels or to keep the motor truck from veering off of the roadway. *U.S. Army Corps of Engineers, Seattle District*

In the late 1930s, Mack offered a "Mack, Jr." line of medium-weight trucks. They actually were built by Reo. This 1936 Mack, Jr. has a Heil dump body. *The Heil Co.*

This is a 1936 Hug model 95, for off-highway use. *Chuck Rhoads*

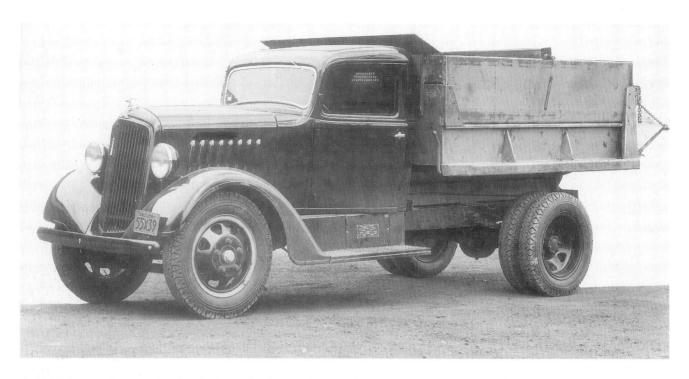

A 1936 Reo with a Hockensmith dump body. *Hockensmith Corp.*

A 1936 Sterling with a dump body used by the Town of Lake Highway Department. Its top sideboard folds down, making it easier to load or unload with hand shovels. *Ernest Sternberg*

Size is relative. This 1936 White gets a ride on a coal excavator in Seelyville, Indiana. *Volvo/White*

The City of Knoxville operated this 1936 Studebaker COE, shown with a dump body carrying a load of debris. *The William F. Harrah Automobile Foundation*

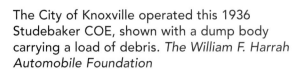

A 1937 Autocar, possibly used as a yard tractor, pulling a new Penn dump body with triple hoists. The Chevrolets on the left are from late 1940s. The headlights on the Autocar are sealed-beam replacements of the original equipment. *Hockensmith Corp.*

This 1937 Dodge has its Heil coal body lifted about as high as coal bodies go. Note that a single piston thrusts into the center of "closed scissors," forcing them open. *The Heil Co.*

A mid-1930s Ford dump truck being turned on a turntable at Scotts Bluff National Monument. *Scotts Bluff National Monument*

A 1937 Studebaker pulls a Heil dump body on a semitrailer, used in Oshkosh, Wisconsin. *The Heil Co.*

A 1937 Sterling with a Heil rock body. Note both the truck's chain drive, and the head lamp protectors. *The Heil Co.*

A 1938 Available with twin rear axles and a large dump body. *National Automotive History Collection, Detroit Public Library*

A pair of circa 1938 Brockways with dump bodies installed by the Mayer Body Corporation of Pittsburgh, for use by a contractor in Edgeworth, Pennsylvania. *Mayer Body Corp.*

A circa 1938 Dodge COE, with a dump body. *Baker Library, Harvard University*

Use of a spreader on a farm field. Two workers are feeding lime into the spreader with shovels. The dump body lacks a small chute door in the rear, which probably could feed the spreader. However, this was the Depression, and labor was cheap. *American Automobile Manufacturers Assn.*

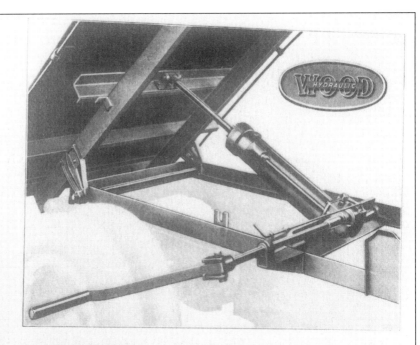

MODEL "A" HYDRAULIC HAND OPERATED HOIST

THE Model "A" is a hydraulic hoist, similar in principle to power operated hydraulic hoists. It is simple and safe to operate. There are no ratchets, catches, dogs or brakes. The hoist "holds" automatically when the crank is stopped, the load resting on a solid column of oil, with a hydraulic cushioning effect. The body comes down when valve is turned. It is impossible for crank to "fly back" or "kick" operator. When not in use, the crank folds under the body. Hoist is of steel construction throughout. Moving parts operate in oil, so that wear is reduced to a minimum. Dumping angle is 45°. Weight, 300 lbs. Maximum capacity, 2 tons.

Price, hoist only . . . . $97.00 f. o. b. Detroit, not installed.

See other side for WOOD dump bodies used with the Model "A" Hoist.
For power-operated hoists, see Bulletin No. 7.

GAR WOOD INDUSTRIES, INC.
7924 Riopelle Street   -   -   -   Detroit, Michigan

Trade journal ad for a Gar Wood hydraulic hoist in the late 1930s.
National Automotive History Collection, Detroit Public Library

A 1938 White cabover makes a coal delivery. Short-wheelbase trucks were easier to maneuver and were less likely to block traffic. Also, coal trucks were "spot-checked" by having to drive to city scales where the weight of the loaded truck was matched against the truck's empty weight plus the weight of coal it was carrying as evidenced by the invoices made out for deliveries yet to be made. Many city scales had been installed at the time of horse-drawn coal wagons and they were short, requiring larger coal trucks to be weighed twice, first the front axle, then the rear axle(s). Short-wheelbase coal trucks fit more easily on the short scales. *Volvo/White*

This 1939 Autocar is pulling a trailer with a Gar Wood dumping body. *National Automotive History Collection, Detroit Public Library*

A late 1930s Hendrickson with a single-piston Heil dump body. *The Heil Co.*

This is a late 1930s Reo with a Heil twin-piston dump body. *The Heil Co.*

This is a 1940 Studebaker with a dump body, carrying a load of coal. *National Automotive History Collection, Detroit Public Library*

A circa 1940 Hendrickson with dump body installed by Auto Truck. *Auto Truck*

HERCULES STEEL PRODUCTS Co

This ad for Hercules dump bodies appeared in a 1940 issue of *Chevrolet Dealer News. American Automobile Manufacturers Assn.*

This is a 1939 International COE tractor with a dump body mounted on a Fruehauf trailer. *American Automobile Manufacturers Assn.*

Right & Below: A late 1930s Brockway with a body that dumps to the driver's left. Longhand notation on the photo said "double bottom 1-1/2-inch oak lining between." *Hockensmith Corp.*

This 1939 Ford dump truck with twin rear axles was used in Freeport, Illinois. *Auto Truck*

A Heil rock body on a late 1930s International. *The Heil Co.*

This is a highly customized 1940 Chevrolet COE painted orange with a flame treatment in front. It is owned by Barbara and Bob Zahn.

The flatbed lifts with a dump mechanism. The front of the bed is cut out to accommodate the power plant. Photos were taken in Washington State in 1999.

A 1939 White used by the Great Lakes Coal & Dock Company, in Milwaukee. This must be its first day on the job. *Great Lakes Coal & Dock Co.*

Chapter 5
1941–1950

The Call to War

This was the decade of World War II. Dump trucks were busy on both the battle front and on the home front. The army used dump trucks in many of its construction projects, such as the Burma Road or Air Corps strips. At home, new military facilities and factories to support the war effort were being built everywhere. The steel industry required massive tonnages of iron ore, coke, and limestone. With most cars and trucks gone to the war effort, this was also a decade of innovation for people like farmers, who still needed big machinery for their work.

The Agricultural Experiment Station at South Dakota State College in Brookings issued a bulletin describing how farmers could fashion a four-wheel rubber-tire trailer out of an old auto chassis and a frame. Each trailer used a chassis on the bottom and a frame on top, with a hydraulic auto bumper jack installed in the center, front, between the two. The wagon box, which attached to the upper frame, could be lifted in front with the jack for dumping, while the bottom frame, with four wheels and tires, remained on the ground.

This is a 1941 Autocar powered by a Cummins diesel. The dump trailer was built by Utility Trailer Sales Co. The rig was used in San Jose, California. *Watson & Meehan, San Francisco*

In 1942 an auto industry trade group, the Automotive Council for War Production, reviewed development of trucks used in specific industries vital to the war effort, including mining, road construction, and coal delivery. The group's findings are summarized below:

- Mining placed three unusual stresses on the large dump trucks. First, the heavy load was dropped into the truck in one motion, straining the body, frame, axles, and tires. Often a rock guard was provided at the front of the dump body to protect the cab. Second, the roads were rough, requiring high clearance and special protection for the bottom of the oil pan. Third, in many mines, the loaded trucks had to make a slow, steep climb out of the pit.

- Road building placed additional requirements on dump trucks, including scoop end dump bodies, since tailgates were often damaged by the steam shovel loading the truck; backup brakes to prevent trucks from rolling backward in excavation work; armored front ends to protect the radiator; higher gear reduction; additional frame supports; and a second rear driving axle.

- Coal delivery trucks benefited from the introduction of short wheelbase, cab-over-engine models, which were more maneuverable in urban areas. The high-lift coal bodies increased the length of chutes that could be employed. Both improvements reduced manpower needs.

The report also summarized other developments in trucks over two decades (1922–1942) comparing a 1922 Pierce-Arrow and a 1941 Dodge, both with dump bodies. The Dodge had a chassis weight (the weight of the truck without passengers or load) that was 3,000 pounds less and a payload that was 1,500 pounds more; pneumatic rather than solid tires; four-wheel hydraulic brakes rather than two-wheel mechanical brakes; and a speed of 40 to 50 miles per hour rather than only 15.

Diesel power for trucks had been introduced in the 1930s and widely used during World War II. After the war, diesels began replacing gasoline engines in many applications requiring large power plants. Dump trucks fit into this category. Diesels were specified for new equipment and also were used to replace gasoline-powered engines in existing trucks. Cummins Diesel Company published a quarterly magazine, *The Dependable Diesel,* for dealers, customers, and potential customers that included stories of various users who had switched to Cummins diesel engines. Some examples

An early 1940s Federal COE with twin rear axles and a Hercules dump body. *Perfection Cobey*

Two views of Heil dump bodies on a 1941 Dodge chassis, showing how the tailgate and sides can be lowered into a flatbed position. *The Heil Co.*

The tailgate apparently can swing from either the top or bottom. *The Heil Co.*

The truck is a 1941 Ford with a Heil body that was built to handle refuse boxes. It can collect a box by backing under it and lifting it off the ground. It leaves a box in a reverse manner. It can also dump the contents of the box it's carrying, as shown here. *The Heil Co.*

A 1941 International with a lifted coal body in horizontal position. Above the cab in front of the body appears to be a hoist for raising its front. The truck was used in Milwaukee. *The Heil Co.*

of Cummins-powered, or repowered, dump trucks mentioned in a 1946 issue include two Euclids used by a North Carolina gravel company; a repowered Bulldog Mack used by a sand and stone company in New York City; a fleet of Sterlings used in the Pennsylvania coal fields; Euclids used by a stone quarry in North Carolina; a Walter pulling a bottom dump-trailer in a mine near Jasonville, Indiana; and Macks and Euclids used in the Mesabi Iron Range in Minnesota.

At the war's end, the economy boomed and a wave of highway and home construction expanded the market for dump trucks. With labor scarce and relatively expensive, truck drivers had to be more productive. Contractors would hire fewer helpers to assist with unloading trucks.

To increase a truck's capacity, a few firms offered "second rear axle" kits. The "Load-Booster" device had a lengthened propeller shaft that allowed the driving axle to be moved further back. The new, third axle was placed in front of the existing drive axle. It was not powered, although it had brakes. The alleged advantage of having the driving axle at the rear was that when the truck was headed uphill, any load shift would be over the rear, driving axle. Secondly, the wheels on the front of the two rear axles were said to help "clear the path" for the driven wheels that followed. The "Load-Booster" was built in Detroit by the Detroit Automotive Products Corporation. The same firm offered the Thornton double rear axle kit, which had a differential that fit between the two rear axles and powered them both. Little Giant Products of Peoria built and sold an axle kit that added a nonpowered axle to the rear. (In 1946 Little Giant also offered two hand hoists for dump bodies. One fit under the body and relied on gear wheels; the vertical model fit behind the cab and used a hand crank and chain.)

The Anthony Company manufactured a full line of dump bodies in the postwar era. Its sales literature covers a range of hoists and bodies. The piston on its smallest hoist was 6 inches in diameter; larger cylinders were 7 or 8 inches. Larger hoists were produced by linking two hoists together. The firm offered eight body styles, including two garbage bodies on straight chassis. The length of the piston stroke was 20 inches on the smaller models and 24 inches of the larger models.

The Anthony bodies were built on two frames, hinged at the rear. The top frame held the dump body, while the lower frame (which shared length and width dimensions with most truck frames) would be attached to the truck chassis frame. According to the Anthony literature, this made it relatively easy to shift the entire mechanism to a new truck. Dump bodies were also sold for farm use. Their top angle of lift was 45 degrees rather than 55 degrees, the maximum angle for the other bodies.

All the Anthony hoists described so far were underbody hoists. Anthony also offered for farm use a dump body raised by a vertical hydraulic hoist mounted right behind the cab, similar to the vertical hoists of World War I vintage. Capacity for the hoists decreased as body length increased. Thus, for one hoist, lifting capacity with a 9-foot body was 30 tons; a 12-foot body, 22 tons; and a 15-foot body, 18 tons. Anthony also worked with Trailmobile, a trailer manufacturer, to build and market a twin-axle semitrailer with a dump body.

Other literature indicates that Anthony bodies could be fitted on other makes of full and semitrailers. Anthony offered several sizes of a lime-spreader body. The hopper had a V-bottom running lengthwise with a conveyor belt that would feed the product to the spreader.

Two other Anthony brochures covered dump bodies for light trucks, 1-1/2- to 2-ton capacity, and coal trucks. The market for coal trucks would start shrinking, as most homeowners preferred burning either oil or gas. However, at the time of the brochure (1948), Anthony

The Town of Hamden used this 1942 GMC with a Heil dump body. *The Heil Co.*

A Hercules Road Spreader, built to follow a dump body. It's powered by an independent motor. *Blackhawk Classic Auto Collection*

was offering 56 different coal bodies, ranging from 5- to 15-ton capacity.

A 1950 publication of the *American City Magazine* showed various spreaders and sanders that trailed the rear-dump body. A departure from this design was the "Roadsaver," built by Gabb Manufacturing Company of Gabb, Connecticut. The body held the spreader and the spreader operator at the front of the dump truck. A long frame ran underneath the truck and extended beyond the front of the truck. A conveyer carried the materials forward the length of the truck to the spreader. This was a three-man operation, consisting of the truck driver, the spreader operator in front, and a man standing at the rear of the dump body to regulate the flow of materials onto the forward-moving belt.

In 1950, the National Lift Company of Waukesha, Wisconsin, was offering a "Dump-O-Matic" twin-hoist mechanism for small (1-ton) chassis. The brochure said the "Dump-O-Matic is designed for Chevrolet, Diamond-T, Dodge, Ford, G.M.C., International, Studebaker, and Willys pickup trucks." The hydraulic pump that powered the hoist was carried under the hood, and driven by the truck's fan belt. The truck's standard pickup box could be used or others could be provided. The company also offered a higher top box that could be placed inside the pickup box and bolted in within 15 minutes. This gave much higher sides and also was flared out over the rear wheels. It was for hauling ashes or leaves.

A 1942 Chevrolet COE with a Penn dump body. The body has rope hoops and rings for securing a tarpaulin. *Hockensmith Corp.*

Aluminum producers expanded capacity during World War II and, at the war's end, sought new markets for their product. One potential customer was the transportation industry, in which lighter materials would result in fuel savings by reducing overall vehicle weights. In the late 1940s, the Auto Truck Equipment Company of Pittsburgh built some aluminum dump bodies. Although the bodies required special welding, the lower weight allowed users to increase their payloads.

An early 1940s Federal dump truck working in the mud. *National Archives*

This shows a Heil slant-type hoist under construction, as it is placed on a mid-1940s Chevrolet. Two pistons lift the entire body vertically, and a third piston dumps the body. *The Heil Co.*

A 1942 GMC with a Penn body and cab shield. *Hockensmith Corp.*

A 1942 Diamond-T with a Penn body and hoist, coal door and chute, and a cab shield. *Hockensmith Corp.*

A Heil dump trailer pulled by a military Diamond-T 6x6 chassis during World War II. *The Heil Co.*

A war-surplus truck, probably a Chevrolet, used by the airport in Tucson, Arizona. *Tucson Airport Authority*

A side-dumping Heil body on a World War II Army chassis, probably a Studebaker. *The Heil Co.*

This looks like a war-surplus Federal painted in civilian colors. The buyer was the Sunnyhill Mining Co. The twin-hoist Penn body is by Hockensmith and is 15 feet long. The sides are 45 inches high, "straight up to 18 inches then flare, then up to 45 inches." Penn Body literature in the early 1940s said: "Penn telescopic hoists assure you of adequate strength—no small piston rods and lifting mechanisms to wear, bend or twist under load. The lifting power is applied direct to the load without the use of rollers, arms, levers or cams; therefore, less working parts, less weight and a lower upkeep. You can't have trouble with parts that aren't there." The largest single-piston hoist that Penn offered could lift 25 tons 57 inches. The four piston sleeves were of 11-1/2-inch, 9-3/8-inch, 8-inch, and 7-inch diameters. The literature also said: "PENN Hoists are lighter in weight than any other of equal lifting capacity. This is especially true of models . . . which weigh up to 500 pounds less than competitive units. PENN Hoists are much more economical in oil consumption. Drivers tell us that they have operated PENN Hoists for seven years without any addition of oil." *Hockensmith Corp.*

This war-surplus Studebaker had a new dump body installed at the Hockensmith plant in Penn, Pennsylvania. In the background are two Dodge chassis. *Hockensmith Corp.*

A Euclid off-highway dump truck from the 1940s. *Billy Green*

This close-up shows the body raised. *Kranz-built Bodies*

This 1945 International K-3 with a Marion 2-yard dump body was sold in Lima, Ohio. *Kranz-built Bodies*

A World War II surplus chassis, probably a White, with an Auto Truck-installed dump body, used for coal. Sign at rear warns following motorists: "Danger Air Brakes." *Auto Truck*

An ad for war surplus White half-tracks, noting that a dump body "can easily be installed." *American Automobile Manufacturers Assn.*

A 1946 Available with an Auto Truck body, used for carrying coal. *Auto Truck*

Corn is transferred from a truck to a storage silo. The truck is a mid-1940s Chevrolet. The front of the entire truck is lifted by a manual hoist. The device that elevates the corn is powered by the farm tractor's PTO. *Deere & Co. Archives*

A World War II-era White, probably war surplus, outfitted with a Penn body. *Hockensmith Corp.*

An early 1940s heavy-duty Dodge, working in California. *Library, University of California, Davis*

Dodge trucks were sold as Fargo trucks in Canada. This 1946 Fargo with a dump body was parked too close to a fire, and its windows are broken. *City of Ottawa Archives*

Note the details in the Penn body mounted on a 1946 Dodge chassis. The chute door in the rear is for coal. Both trucks have grille guards. *Hockensmith Corp.*

This 1947 photo shows a Ford with a snowplow used in Virginia. The outside crank elevates the blade. Barely visible is a rod sticking out to the right (as we are positioned) of the parking light, apparently to let the driver know the clearance of the blade. On top of the blade at the left of the photo is a small marker device to let the driver know how far the blade extends. The truck has a dump body and on its side is a rack for transporting the temporary signs one often sees at the site of road maintenance work. *Virginia Department of Highways and Transportation*

The City of West Bend, Wisconsin, had a Heil body installed on this 1946 FWD chassis. *The Heil Co.*

Hockensmith rock body on a half-track tractor, circa 1946, built using surplus military equipment. The operator's seat and steering wheel are on this side of the engine. *Hockensmith Corp.*

A war-surplus half-track converted to a wet concrete hauler. *Portland Cement Association*

This 1947 Ford with a dumping stake body is shown with both the body and the hood raised. It's owned by Allen Fisher of Maryland. *Allen M. Fisher*

The drive shaft and the PTO-shaft (at the top), which powers the hoist. *Allen M. Fisher*

Below: Close-up of bolts connecting hoist frame and truck frame. Note board in between. *Allen M. Fisher*

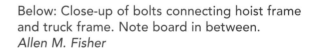

Left: This shows the hoist piston, lifting arms, and rollers. *Allen M. Fisher*

Rear view of the body, which Mr. Fisher rebuilt. *Allen M. Fisher*

Above: The hoist piston, fully extended. *Allen M. Fisher*

The safety rod is in the stored position. It's used when the body is raised and one wishes to work under it. Below it we see the timber between the frames of the truck and the dump body. *Allen M. Fisher*

Right: The mechanism on this side of the piston is the "up/down" rod. *Allen M. Fisher*

A Penn body mounted on a circa 1947 International model KB14F chassis, one of the heavier chassis built by International. The truck was sold to a coal company. *Hockensmith Corp.*

A late 1940s Studebaker with grain body, lifted by a St. Paul hoist, used in Montana. *The Smithsonian Institution*

A Galion body installed on a late 1940s Mack by the Mayer Body Corporation of Pittsburgh. Company records indicate that the body weighed 1,775 pounds, and the hoist, 975 pounds. In building the body, 12-gauge steel was used in the floor and rear, and 14-gauge in the sides and front. *Mayer Body Corp.*

A circa 1947 Sterling, still with chain drive, with a Penn rock body. Note that both headlights and front turn indicator are shielded. *Hockensmith Corp.*

A late 1940s International with a full load of coal. *Amax Coal Co.*

A garbage body dumps to empty. The chassis is a 1940s Autocar, and the rig was used in New York City. In front is both a guard grille and a snowplow mount. *City of New York Department of Sanitation*

A 1948–1950 Ford with body installed by Auto Truck Equipment Sales in Chicago. The dump body has a cab protector. *Auto Truck*

This is a Euclid, from the later 1940s, used in Mesabi iron ore mines in Minnesota. *Watson & Meehan, San Francisco*

A late 1940s Chevrolet with a single-piston hoist and dump body. *Monon Trailer*

A dump hoist lifts the pickup body on a small Ford, circa 1949. *James K. Wagner*

A 1949 GMC cabover with a dump body and cab guard, purchased by Consolidated Edison. *Consolidated Edison*

Above & Below: A short dump body on a 1949 Kenworth chassis. Body dumps to the side as well. *Paccar*

A 1949 Mack off-highway dump truck.
National Archives

An experimental Sterling off-highway dump truck,
built in 1949. It has a Heil body.
Ernest Sternberg

One does not associate sleeper cabs with dump
bodies. This circa 1949 White was originally a
highway tractor that pulled semitrailers. A
subsequent owner installed a dump body.

A side-dumping Penn body on a 1950 Mack. *Hockensmith Corp.*

This type of body carried pulpwood that would be dumped into troughs at the paper mill. For repetitive deliveries, side dumping is faster than having to back up. *Hockensmith Corp.*

If this circa 1950 Sterling lost a wheel, one would wonder what had happened to the vehicle with which it collided. Tow truck was based in Hartford, Connecticut. *Steve Ritchie*

A circa 1950 International with an OBECO farm body that can be dumped. *Omaha Body & Equipment Co.*

Chapter 6

1951–1960

Postwar Boom

World War II was over, but the nation was fighting another war in Korea. Both war and peacetime demands kept industry busy. Later in the decade, the United States began construction of its Interstate Highway System, one of the most significant and largest building projects ever undertaken. Building this system, which stretched into subsequent decades, created unprecedented demand for dump trucks, scrapers, loaders, and earthmoving equipment.

In his 1951 book, *Automotive and Construction Equipment*, C. W. Lindgren made a number of observations about dump trucks and their use:

> *Dump truck operations are in most sections of the country seasonal or intermittent. This tends to*

A 1951 Autocar, used by a fertilizer company in Bryn Mawr, Pennsylvania. The 25-yard dump body and trailer were both built by Fruehauf. *Watson & Meehan, San Francisco*

discourage the ownership of large fleets of dump trucks for providing service to others. In general, it is difficult to operate dump trucks profitably because the equipment is subject to abuse, business is by competitive price, and service provided to others is usually of short duration—one part of a large contract.

Dump trucks can be operated profitably when there is an abundance of work to be done like on large contracts involving long hauls. Contractors engaged in road surfacing usually have efficient fleets of dump trucks or they sublet contracts for hauling materials like sand, gravel asphalt, and concrete batches. Dump trucks are used in the construction of sewerage systems, bridges, industrial sites and many other kinds of projects where dirt has to be hauled away and materials brought in.

The Cummins Diesel Company's quarterly magazine, *The Dependable Diesel*, mentioned in the previous chapter, describes various diesel engine applications. Diesel dump truck applications from this decade include a diesel-powered Dart with a bottom-dumping

trailer used in an underground mine in Oklahoma. The diesel engine was "equipped to eliminate carbon monoxide. The unit carries an oxygen cylinder from which pure oxygen is piped to the exhaust manifold of the engine where it mixes with the escaping gases, leaving the exhaust clear and odorless. The use of this system makes the operation of Cummins Diesels underground acceptable to state mining boards."

A fleet of seven twin-engine Euclid rear-dump trucks was used to haul 9 million tons of rock for a 4,800-foot causeway, 80 feet wide and 14 feet above high tide between Nova Scotia and Cape Breton. According to the article, "Giant electric shovels load the Euclids with upward of 43 tons of rock at Porcupine Hill and then the load is carried down a rough haul road, through the granite muck of the causeway to the outer extremity, where the boulders are dumped. . . . Three shifts of drivers are assigned to these Cummins-powered 'brutes,' and they in turn push these trucks 24 hours a day, six days a week. Only on Sundays are the trucks taken to Northern Construction Company's garage where they are completely serviced."

A Dart, used in a coal mining operation. *Amax Coal Co.*

This 1951 International has a Penn body that can be enclosed by adding sideboards. *Hockensmith Corp.*

A booklet, apparently prepared jointly by the Euclid Road Machinery Company and Cummins Diesel Engine Company in 1953, describes a range of Euclid equipment available with Cummins power. Five Cummins engines were used with horsepower of 165, 175, 200, 275, and 300. All of the Euclid equipment was intended for off-road use. The smallest Euclid dump truck pictured was twice the height of the driver standing alongside. This rig carried 15 tons, and dumped to the rear. Its front tire size was 12.00x24 and its rear tires were 14.00x24. Another version of the same size model came with a 10-speed, rather than 5-speed, transmission, hydraulic booster steering and larger tires, 13.00x24 front and 16.00x25 rear. The next size of rear-dump trucks could carry 22 tons. Their power trains were designed for carrying heavy loads up steep grades and their tire sizes were 14.00x24 front and 18.00x25 rear. The largest rear-dump Euclid carried 34 tons and was powered by two Cummins 200-horsepower engines mounted side by side. It had twin rear axles and 16.00x25 tires, front and rear. Seven models of tractor-drawn bottom-dumping semitrailers were offered, with capacities

from 20 to 50 tons. The larger ones were all intended for carrying coal in open mines. The Euclid booklet also included scrapers and loaders.

A 1954 report of the Hydraulic Hoist and Steel Dump Body Manufacturers Association listed these members: Anthony, Converto, Cresci, Daybrook, Galion, Gar Wood, Heil, Hercules, Leach, Marion, Perfection, and Truck Engineering Co. The Converto Manufacturing Company was located in Cambridge, Indiana, and Cresci Body Company was in Vineland, New Jersey. Daybrook Hydraulic Corporation was in Bowling Green, Ohio. Gar Wood was in Wayne, Michigan, and Hercules was now located in Galion, Ohio. The Leach Company was—and is—located in Oshkosh, Wisconsin, and manufactures primarily garbage bodies. The Truck Engineering Company was in Fort Wayne, Indiana.

Some reports from the Truck Trailer Manufacturers Association told of U.S. truck trailer (presumably both semi and full) production during this period. In 1954, 55,339 trailers were produced, of which 1,090 were dump trailers. By 1960, the numbers climbed to 62,021 and 1,418 respectively.

An early 1950s International with a dump body discharging into a spreader. *Deere & Co. Archives*

Below: Special bodies were needed for "dumping" bricks, because the bricks could not drop very far without breaking. It was advantageous to keep the stacks intact, rather than have them scatter. Here's another way to haul bricks: a straddle carrier. The tractor is an early 1950s Kenworth and the load is cement blocks. The carrier straddles the entire load, lifts it, and transports it to its destination, where it's lowered to the ground. *Challenge Cook Bros.*

This is a 1951 Mack with a dump body, operated by a Chicago contractor. *Press Tank & Equipment Co., Chicago*

Mid West Body, of Paris, Illinois, built many bodies intended for use by farmers, and used the term "grain tight" to describe their construction. The literature indicated that their steel underframing was designed so that a hoist could be fitted between their bottom frame and the truck's chassis, without increasing the body's overall height.

Weight limits continued to challenge the industry. In order to carry more weight, operators placed the load toward the front of the truck, since the front axle usually was not loaded to the limit. A Galion sales manual from the 1950s said: "The habit of forward loading has grown from the fact that in cases where state weight laws are rigidly enforced, it is usually very much more difficult to get legal capacity onto the front truck axle. The fines assessed on truck operators are usually the result of overloaded rear axle or axles… So that in many cases our customer piles his payload on the front end of the body, in some cases to the extreme that he even loads his cab protector, and his payload does not extend very much higher than floor level in the rear." From an equipment design and operation standpoint, forward loading required more lifting capacity from the hoist than would an evenly distributed load.

This is a detail in a Hockensmith rock-carrying body. It's an oak timber that acts as a shock absorber between the body longitudinals and the main frame members of the truck chassis. These timbers help absorb the blows of large loads of rocks dumped into the bed. They were called "wood sleepers," and would have to be replaced from time to time during the life of the truck. Just above the center of the photo is the hinge. *Hockensmith Corp.*

Above and Below: A 1952 Autocar with Gar Wood hoists and side-dumping compartment, used by a Southern California cement company. The trailer was built by Fruehauf. *Volvo/White*

A circa 1952 Diamond-T with a Penn body, built by Hockensmith. *Hockensmith Corp.*

Below: Unloading a coal truck in the early 1950s. The coal is dropped onto a conveyor belt that carries it to the sidewalk opening. Will the owner of the white Caddy convertible notice coal dust on his car? *National Coal Association*

Above: A circa 1951 Reo loading gravel. *American Automobile Manufacturers Assn.*

This picture showing an early 1950s Mack was originally accompanied by a 1952 press release from Jones & Laughlin Steel Corporation, which said: "Two-and-a-half yard shovel drops about five tons per shovelful of jagged rock diggings into E. F. Robinson Company truck working on the Penn-Lincoln Parkway job in Pittsburgh, under contract to B. Perini and Sons, Framingham, Mass. Robinson trucks were fabricated of J&L Otiscoloy high-strength steel and Jailoy heat-treated plate by the Penn Body Division of the Hockensmith Corporation, Penn, Pa." *Jones & Laughlin Steel Corporation*

After World War II, International built a heavier-duty model, sometimes called the "Western" or the "Emeryville" model. This one, from the early 1950s, has the side of its hood removed to improve cooling and it's pulling a large body, probably too large for use on a highway. At right we see another rig climbing a hill. *Challenge Cook Bros.*

Three workers shoveling salted sand from a dump truck that has a snowplow blade in front and a mechanical spreader on the rear. *Pennsylvania Turnpike Commission*

This early 1950s Walter has a 12-cubic-yard Penn mining dump body built by Hockensmith. It's lifted by twin telescopic hoists. Walter ads of this era showed similar trucks working in Minnesota's Mesabi iron mines. *Hockensmith Corp.*

This 1952 photo shows blast furnace slag being loaded with a clamshell shovel into an early 1950s White with a Hockensmith body. The original caption said that the body was made of Jones & Laughlin "Otiscoloy" steel, apparently necessary because of slag's abrasive and corrosive qualities. *Jones & Laughlin Steel Corporation*

The U.S. Army used this early 1950s International dump with a cab protector. *U.S. Army Transportation Museum, Fort Eustis*

Two views of a side-dumping body pulled by a 1953 Autocar. The owner was a quarry in Summit, New Jersey. Note that the body is lifted by a hooking device hanging from the overhead tower. A similar rig waits in the rear. *Volvo/White*

A 1953 Autocar off-highway dump truck. Its body was rated at 27 yards. Note the round hole near the top of the raised body. When the body is lowered, the truck's exhaust feeds into this hole. The warm exhaust then circulates between the layers of the body, keeping the contents from freezing to the body's surface. *Volvo/White*

The Cleveland Electric Illuminating Company used this 1953 Autocar with bottom-dump coal trailers. *Volvo/White*

Opposite: It's shown dumping; apparently it dumps to one side only. While a hydraulic piston is visible, it may also be lifted by an outside device (note top of picture). *Volvo/White*

An Easton side-dump body pulled by a 1953 Autocar. It was used at a cement plant in Fairborn, Ohio. *Volvo/White*

This is a 27-yard Heil body on an off-highway 1953 Autocar chassis. Note ladder steps up to cab. *Volvo/White*

This off-highway 1953 Autocar chassis carries a 10-yard Marion body. *Volvo/White*

An early 1950s Brockway with a Hockensmith rock body. *Hockensmith Corp.*

A 1953 Diamond-T cabover used in a Chicago suburb. Twin pistons lift the body. *Press Tank & Equipment Co., Chicago*

When elevated, we see that this Brockway (same as pictured above) is lifted by twin pistons. Note it has no tailgate. *Hockensmith Corp.*

A circa 1953 GMC tractor pulling a semitrailer with two side-dumping compartments. *Hockensmith Corp.*

An early 1950s FWD with a Penn hoist and body. The body was 11 feet long, 7 feet wide, and 21 inches tall. *Hockensmith Corp.*

A trucking company in Dedham, Massachusetts, used this 1954 Autocar. *Volvo/White*

A 1954 Autocar with a half-cab, intended for off-highway use. It was used in Lancaster, Pennsylvania. *Volvo/White*

The Azusa Rock Company in Azusa, Colorado, used this 1954 Autocar with bottom-dumping trailers. Note that these dump at right angles to the road—they could lay a wide strip of materials along a roadway. *Volvo/White*

An off-highway 1954 Autocar working at the Medusa Portland Cement Company in Cleveland. *Volvo/White*

The Autocar press release called this the "Michigan Special" because of all its axles. It was used by a Detroit sand and gravel operator. Its front two tires were larger than the other 36. *Volvo/White*

144

Cook Bros. trucks were built in Los Angeles from 1942 until 1964. This is a 1954 model that looks like the first cousin to a Reo. To the right of the mirror is a turn indicator that would point outward to signal that the driver was turning left. *Challenge Cook Bros.*

Page from a brochure showing a Hendrickson truck and trailer used in a coal strip mining operation. *Hendrickson Mfg. Co.*

Some Diamond-Ts from the early 1950s with side-dumping bodies dumping concrete in a road-building project in Pennsylvania. *Pennsylvania Department of Transportation*

A 1954 Ford with a Press-installed body. *Press Tank & Equipment Co., Chicago*

View under an installed Penn body, focusing on the hinge between the chassis and the body. *Hockensmith Corp.*

Close-up view of a Penn body and hoist in the 1950s. Note that thrust of the hoist is horizontal. A handle at the top releases the tailgate, and a chain at the bottom catches the tailgate as it falls. *Hockensmith Corp.*

A spreader, permanently mounted on a 1950s truck chassis, used in Missouri. *Missouri Highway and Transportation Commission*

One of the group of Coleman H16000, 6 x 6's, recently shipped to So. Africa

All-wheel drive Coleman trucks were built in Littleton, Colorado, from 1925 through 1986. This one, from the mid-1950s, was exported to South Africa. *FABCO*

A tattered 1955 Dodge with dual rear axles. *Mark R. Wayman*

A 1955 Kenworth tractor pulling two high, enclosed bottom-dump trailers. *Paccar*

A 1950s Mack LR, intended for off-highway use, pulling a side-dump trailer. *American Automobile Manufacturers Assn.*

A mid-1950s Walter "snow fighter" used in Pennsylvania. The snowplow mount is in front, and the body feeds down into a spreader at the rear. Note the exhaust pipe bent over the cab. *Pennsylvania Department of Transportation*

Rack on the top of a Penn body for holding a tarpaulin. Note the tooled finish. Some years ago, John Steighner, who worked for Hockensmith, answered the author's query about the burnished bodies. He said that the tooled finish "was done on aluminum bodies only. The method I devised to do this was quite simple. The tool used was the rubber cup from a small sized 'plumber's helper' stuffed with steel wool attached to a 3/8-inch electric drill to rotate the cup. By pressing the steel wool against the aluminum as the drill rotated the cup, multiple circular scratches were made in the aluminum. This was done repeatedly to get the overall effect. It was an expensive operation because it required many man hours to do a body." *Hockensmith Corp.*

The original caption on this photo said: "1956 Cook Bros. Stablilift multistage, single hoist, end dump semitrailer with batch gates." Tractor is a Cook Bros. *Challenge Cook Bros.*

This is a 1956 GMC with dual rear wheels and an 8- to 10-yard Columbia dump box. *The Truck Gazette*

This is a 1956 Cook Bros. Driver sits next to the engine in offset cab. *Challenge Cook Bros.*

A cab-forward 1956 Chevrolet with a Monon dump trailer. *Monon Trailer*

This 1956 Kenworth was powered by electricity so it could work inside a mine. Overhead power lines are similar to those used for streetcars in urban areas. Operator must check for overhead wires before raising the body into dump position. *Paccar*

This is a mid-1950s Mack with a Hockensmith body designed to lift, carry, and dump pots of slag. It's shown on a railroad flatcar, bound for a foundry in Canada. *Hockensmith Corp.*

This is a customized 1956 Ford pickup with a dump body, owned by Darleen and Phil Sicotte. It was spotted in the Pacific Northwest in 1999. The pickup body is lifted by twin pistons. The truck is painted purple, and the undercarriage is red.

A late 1950s Mack performing flood control work near Yakima, Washington, in 1966. *U. S. Army Corps of Engineers, Seattle District*

A 1956 Peterbilt on a long wheelbase dumping a long frameless semitrailer, using a long piston. Most telescoping pistons have the largest cylinder on the bottom; this one does not. Advantages of the design shown are that packing covering the collar is on top and less likely to catch grit. Also the widest collar can transmit the most force, and is most useful at the start of the lift. Bracing behind the piston keeps the trailer from going sideways. Photo was taken in California.

A circa 1957 International designed for working in a quarry. *Watson & Meehan, San Francisco*

Above: A 1957 Dodge dump truck, retired in Nevada. *Mark R. Wayman*

Left: This photo, taken in 1962, shows a Dart from the 1950s, used in a coal strip mine. *American Mining Congress*

This is a 1958 Dodge being loaded in a coal yard. Note massive materials handling bridges in the background, needed for transferring coal into the storage area. In the Great Lakes area, huge tonnages of coal were received during the summer months and stockpiled for winter use. When the author was a boy, instruction books for some large erector sets would show models of this equipment. *American Automobile Manufacturers Assn.*

A late 1950s FWD dump truck with a snowplow blade, owned by the Airport Authority in Wichita, Kansas. *Wichita Airport Authority*

A late 1950s GMC. Note that the wooden sideboard is a board that has been split. A board was often used for the top sideboard, as it protected the metal from being dented by loading equipment. Every so often the board would be replaced. *Mark R. Wayman*

This is a circa 1958 International with dual rear axles. *The Truck Gazette*

A late 1950s International spotted at a dirt-loading site in upstate New York. Barely visible behind the rolled-up tarp is the top of a loading conveyer device.

A 1958 Peterbilt with twin rear axles. The hoist is visible on this side of the frame. *FABCO*

This picture was taken when this 1959 Autocar was being sold as a used truck. Its box carried 10 to 12 yards. *The Truck Gazette*

A late 1950s Euclid is in the foreground of this earthmoving process. It will back out onto the filled structure being built out into the water. Two other large pieces of equipment are in the distance. *U. S. Army Corps of Engineers, Walla Walla District*

A nicely restored 1959 Reo, seen from the front. Note there are mud guards (or flaps) both in front of and behind the rear tires. The truck belongs to Gary M. Callis of Maryland. *Gary M. Callis*

Here's a side view. Callis repowered the rig with a Cummins diesel. *Gary M. Callis*

Interior shot shows dash. *Gary M. Callis*

View from behind shows how sideboards and endboards have been added to increase the body's cubic carrying capacity. *Gary M. Callis*

Three views of a 1960 Ford with a Penn trailer body, used by a coal company in Mercer, Pennsylvania. Here we see it loaded with a Hough Payloader. *Hockensmith Corp*

A Lorain excavating shovel is in the background. Man on top of the load is "trimming" it, leveling off the top and filling up the corners. *Hockensmith Corp.*

Dumping the load with a single-piston hoist. *Hockensmith Corp.*

A 1959 Kenworth pulling two bottom-dump trailers. *Paccar*

This 1959 International had its body installed by Jacob Press' sons in Chicago. *Press Tank & Equipment Co., Chicago*

A circa 1960 Walter ore carrier with a bottom-dump trailer. *American Automobile Manufacturers Assn.*

The dump body being pulled by a late 1950s Mack was built by Penn. Note that its sides are lower in the rear than in the front. John Steighner explained that this was to offset the fact that the body was wider at the rear than the front to make it dump easier. The tapering we see offsets this and allows the weight of the load to be evenly distributed, front to rear. *Hockensmith Corp.*

Chapter 7

1961–1970

Highway Building

During this decade work continued on the Interstate Highway System, which employed many dump trucks and other pieces of heavy construction equipment. By 1964, about half of the 41,000-mile system, in terms of mileage, had been completed. Late in the decade, 2,300 miles were added to the system in Appalachia. In 1964 there were 94,732 truck trailers produced in the United States, of which 3,771 were dump trailers. By 1969 the numbers were 171,679 and 4,056, respectively.

In addition, the government established emissions standards for gasoline engines during this decade. At the end of the decade, the federal government created the Environmental Protection Agency (EPA), whose task was to clean up the environment. An early EPA target would be vehicle emissions, especially those coming from diesels. Later, these emission controls would force industries burning coal to switch to coals mined in the West, which were cleaner burning. Western coal is mined in open "strip" mines, a big market for off-highway dump rigs. The nation's concern with environmental protection led to an increased interest in recycling. Most trucks that picked up refuse had dump bodies for emptying; eventually some would need compartments to hold the different categories of materials being recycled.

Trucks at this time incorporated many new and useful features. A number of trucks had integral hood and fender assemblies that could be opened for easier access to the engine. Reinforced fiberglass was used for some hoods and fenders. Manufacturers were also using more aluminum, and more plastic. All of these lighter-weight products allowed the truck to increase its payload. Air suspension seats and air-conditioned cabs became popular with drivers, as might be expected.

Starting in the 1960s the U.S. Census Bureau conducted a "Census of Transportation," which reported in 1967 that there were 15.3 million trucks in the United States, the vast majority of which were small pickups. The 405,000 dump trucks traveled an average of 13,100 miles per year. The dump trucks were also categorized by the industry in which they were used. Over 28 percent of all dump trucks were used in the mining industry, and 13 percent in construction. For-hire uses accounted for 4.5 percent of the dump trucks, and 4.3 percent were used in manufacturing.

The Lectra Haul firm specialized in large off-highway dump trucks. To give an idea of the growth in capacity of its trucks during the decade, its 1961 model could carry 64 tons. The model it introduced in 1963 could carry 85 tons; and its 1965 model could carry 100 tons. Two models were introduced in 1968, one capable of carrying 120 tons, the other, 200 tons. During this same decade, another firm, K-W Dart, built an end-dump truck powered by a 700-horsepower diesel

A 1961 Diamond-T with dumping semitrailer, used by a New Jersey scrap metal dealer. This trailer has a full frame, from which the body is lifted.

that could carry 65 tons. Its cubic capacity was 43 yards level and 55 yards heaped. Mack introduced an off-highway model capable of carrying 50 tons.

Energy Manufacturing Co., Inc. of Monticello, Iowa, offered kits for installing hoists on farmers' grain body trucks. Kits included the upper cylinder yoke mounting assembly, rear hinge and shaft assembly, lower mounting brackets and pivot shaft, telescopic cylinders, sill supports, and hoist guides. The cylinders were mounted on the outsides of the truck's frame. The firm sold hydraulic pumps powered by either the truck's PTO or its 12-volt electrical system. One accessory sold by the company was a body prop to hold the empty body in the raised position when it was being serviced. Energy Manufacturing also offered a hoist for pickups that utilized the pickup body and fenders. The pickup hoist was powered by the pickup's electrical system.

Bartlett Trailer Corporation introduced a dumping hoist for trailers that was mounted inside the tractor's fifth wheel. Marion Metal Products announced a "frameless" dump trailer.

An off-highway 1961 Mack with a Penn twin-hoist dump body. It dwarfs the two men standing in front. *Hockensmith Corp.*

A Euclid off-highway dump truck from the early 1960s. *Mark W. Wayman*

A Hendrickson with two front and two rear axles, from the 1960s.
Hendrickson Mfg. Co.

In a 1967 Paul Newman movie, *Cool Hand Luke*, a 1940s White dump truck had a brief—but heroic—role. In the movie, inmates (the film's "heroes") were attempting to escape from a prison work farm. Using the truck to flee, the escapees raised its dump body (and the bottom-mounted tailgate swung down) to serve as a shield from the fusillade of guards' bullets. (The movie also starred George Kennedy, who received an Oscar for his performance.)

Hercules Galion literature showed bodies "curved" on the interior of both sides, running the length of the body. This design increased the body's cubic capacity. The firm offered 40 different hoists and 29 body models.

"Transfer" truck and trailer arrangements also came into use during this period. The box on the trailer was placed on two large rails and was slightly smaller than the box on the dump truck. To dump the trailer, the trailer was drawn up next to the truck, and then the trailer's box was moved inside the box on the truck, locked into placed, and dumped, using the truck's dumping mechanism. At the dump site, the rig had the maneuverability and traction of a straight truck. These rigs were nicknamed "slam-bangers," because of the noise that the operation generated.

This 1961 GMC is pulling a Trailmobile bottom-dump trailer. *The Truck Gazette*

Here is a 1965 Ford 350 with single rear wheels and an enclosed dump body. *The Truck Gazette*

A short-wheelbase 1962 Kenworth with a dump body and cab protector. *The Truck Gazette*

An early 1960s International with a Heil body and both highway and rail wheels.

A spreader is placed inside the dump body on a circa 1963 International. *American Public Works Association*

This 1965 International was sitting in a used-truck lot. Its 14-foot long body could carry 10 yards. *The Truck Gazette*

A scraper blade is carried under the center of the truck. *American Public Works Association*

This is a 1965 Kenworth tractor with twin bottom-dump, cement-carrying trailers. *The Truck Gazette*

The carrying capacity of this 1965 GMC was increased by installing a Hendrickson dual rear axle. *The Truck Gazette*

A 1960s GMC semitractor pulling two Fruehauf dump trailers in Michigan, where rigs with the largest number of axles could be spotted. This one has 11. *L. E. Reznicek*

A 1966 Chevrolet spotted in Palm Springs, California.

Here's a line of trucks waiting to unload sugar beets in Colorado in 1966. The truck in the foreground appears to be a flatbed carrying a large box, being lifted on the right and dumping to the left. *Bureau of Reclamation, U. S. Department of the Interior*

This 1970 photo shows a 1960s KW Dart hard at work in a coal mine. *National Coal Association*

This is a 1966 Ford F600 with a flatbed dump body. It also has a 12,000-pound winch carried behind the cab. A long rack protects the cab and hood, and there is a toolbox on the side. *The Truck Gazette*

A mid-1960s GMC with a cab protector. It has Nevada plates. *Mark R. Wayman*

This 1967 photograph shows a mid-1960s International with a high body dumping chopped alfalfa into an alfalfa-pellet processing plant in Silt, Colorado. *Bureau of Reclamation, U.S. Department of the Interior*

A 1966 International with twin rear axles and a 10-yard body. *The Truck Gazette*

This is an asphalt spreading operation. Truck is probably a late 1960s Ford. The butane tank is used to fuel heaters that keep the materials more pliable. *Etnyre*

Earl Sherman Co. of Oakland, California, installed this dump body on a 1967 Ford C. Note several horizontal equipment compartments behind the cab. The truck was probably intended for use by a highway maintenance crew. *Earl Sherman*

Above & Below: A large Mack from the 1960s used for strip mining. To judge its size, compare it to the men standing in front. Note how the rear gate opens: it's chained to the chassis frame, and lifts open as the body lifts. *Hockensmith Corp.*

A 10-wheel 1967 International dump truck used in San Jose, California. *The Truck Gazette*

A 16-foot flatbed body with twin-piston dump hoist on a 1968 Chevrolet chassis. *The Truck Gazette*

A 1970 Ford with an 8-yard dump body. *The Truck Gazette*

Two highway workers performing roadside maintenance in Iowa. Their truck is a 1968 Dodge with a snowplow attachment and additional, raised headlights. A warning beacon is on a pole above the cab, and a shovel is on a tool rack between cab and box. There's a tarpaulin covering the box. *Iowa Department of Transportation*

This 1970 Ford F600 has a 15-foot flatbed dumping body. *The Truck Gazette*

This 1968 International carries a 10- to 12-yard dump body. Note cab protector. *The Truck Gazette*

This 1968 Ford F600 has a 12-foot flatbed with a dumping hoist. The front of the body is made of wood and has a window that lines up with the rear window in the cab. *The Truck Gazette*

A 1969 Kenworth with a dump body and a transfer trailer. Both dump bodies were built by Utility. The box on transfer trailers is slightly smaller than the box on the dump truck. The trailer is drawn up next to the rear of the truck and the trailer's box is moved inside the truck's empty box. It is then dumped, making use of the truck-mounted hoist. *The Truck Gazette*

This is a 1968 White Freightliner with a tilting half-cab. Note rails under the dump body; the truck probably picked up and delivered dumpster-like boxes. *The Truck Gazette*

This 1969 Ford carries an 8 to 10-yard dump body on its twin rear axles. *The Truck Gazette*

Spreading gravel in South Carolina. Following motorists should keep some distance behind to avoid "pings." An OSHA inspector might have some comments to make about this operation. *South Carolina Department of Highways and Public Transportation*

Here's a circa 1970 Diamond-Reo. Diamond-Reo trucks were built by the company formed through the consolidation of Diamond-T and Reo. *Mark R. Wayman*

The 16-foot aluminum dump body on this 1970 GMC carries 10 to 12 yards.
The Truck Gazette

A 1970 International pulling a semi and a full trailer that dump through the bottom. Openings are parallel to the road and would be dropped in a windrow. Other machines might be needed to spread the material across the roadway. In distant rear, similar rigs are being loaded at the excavation site. *American Trucking Associations*

A 1970 Kenworth dump truck with twin rear axles. *The Truck Gazette*

A Mack off-highway earthmover, called the "Mack Pack." Note second engine in the rear. *Mack Trucks*

Chapter 8

1971–1980

Innovations Continue

Several fuel crises occurred during the decade, driving the price of gasoline and diesel fuel higher, and causing spot shortages. The economics of truck operation changed to place more emphasis on fuel economy. This decade also ushered in major improvements in truck and trailer braking systems.

Some manufacturers developed flatbed bodies specifically for carrying farm equipment. These bodies employed hoists in the front and had sufficient rear overhang that the back of the bed touched the ground when the front was elevated. This design used a horizontal piston that pushed rearward until the body would start to tilt. A cable with pulleys at the front and rear of the bed would control its descent. When reversed the cable would lift the body and pull it forward into riding position. When the device was in tilted position, the farm equipment could be driven or winched onto the bed, which would then be leveled. Equipment-carrying semitrailers were developed that worked on the same principle.

This 1971 Chevrolet has a 16-foot flatbed body. *The Truck Gazette*

A 5- to 6-yard Euclid body is mounted on this 1971 Chevrolet chassis. *The Truck Gazette*

A Euclid body with a twin-piston hoist carried on a 1971 Ford Louisville chassis. *The Truck Gazette*

Dump trailer literature from a Fruehauf subsidiary, Hobbs Trailers of Fort Worth, addresses the trailer frame lengths and axle spacing necessary to meet some states' weight and axle-spacing regulations. At the trailer's front, an "extended gooseneck permits trailer to be longer to gain the advantage of greater payload legal weight ratings under bridge formula restrictions." ("Bridge" formulas deal with spacing between axles.) The flyer also listed 27 commodities and their respective angles of repose, although the flyer made no specific mention of how the buyer would use this information when buying a dump trailer. Compact earth had the highest angle, 50 degrees. Some Bartlett trailer literature from the same era shows a "lifting 5th wheel" that was placed at the rear of a truck-tractor in the same site as a conventional fifth wheel. This fifth wheel would then lift the trailer's front upward nearly 6 feet. It was designed for dumping prefab housing sections, lumber, ripened citrus fruits, and apples. The device was available with lifts of 12, 14, 18, 24, 36, 48, and 57 inches. Bartlett also made a "Snorkel" fifth wheel device that lifted over 14 feet. Several pictures showed it dumping grain. Peabody Galion literature from this period shows smaller dump bodies with hoists that were powered by the truck's 12-volt electrical system.

Clement Industries of Minden, Louisiana, claimed to have acquired the rights to build "Garwood" hoists and offered a line of dump semitrailers and "pups." Clement built a dumping frame for handling interchangeable containers carrying refuse and scrap, and also sold bottom-dump trailers. The gates below the trailer were opened by air unless the operator wanted to do some "spot" filling, in which case individual gates could be opened manually. Dunham Manufacturing Company was located in Minden at the same time and offered semitrailer and pup trailer dump units.

The Hydraulics Unlimited Manufacturing Co. of Eaton, Colorado, marketed the Harsh hoist. The company's literature shows some of its hoists on lumber bodies, with individual loads of strapped lumber. A line of Harsh dump bodies was also offered. During dumping, the Harsh hoist kept the centerline of the body over the centerline of the truck chassis, for greater stability and lower stress as the load shifted. Freeman Truck Bodies of LaSalle, Colorado, used Harsh hoists for its line of side-dumping bodies, and its literature showed the Freeman Beet Body in action, dumping a load of sugar beets to the truck's left side.

Crysteel Mfg. Inc. of Lake Crystal, Minnesota, offered a bottom-dumping grain body. This company's advertising said, "The Grain Drain saves hundreds and hundreds of pounds for two important reasons. First, it eliminates the need (and the cost) of a hoist. Second, it has no 'platform' or longsills. The sheet metal hopper bottom is bolted directly to the truck frame, and it depends on the truck to be its 'frame'." The body could dump its load of grain within one minute. Crysteel also offered an accompanying bottom dump pup. It sold other styles of dump bodies, many intended for use in the agricultural sector.

The Flow Boy, built in Norman, Oklahoma, was a hopper body with a horizontal chain conveyer that fed the materials to the rear. The body could fit on either a truck or a trailer chassis, and the conveyer could be powered by either the truck or an independent engine. Advantages were reduced stress on the frame and tires, since the load discharged evenly, rather than being suddenly dumped to the rear.

Additionally, the Flow Boy eliminated problems with heights. (Promotional literature showed pictures of conventional dump trailers that had been blown over in an elevated position, or were unable to deliver a smooth flow of materials on a highway surfacing project because of an overpass.) The main use of the Flow Boy equipment appeared to be placing a uniform windrow of gravel along the roadway as part of a paving project.

In January 1979, Mack announced that it was ceasing production of its large off-highway vehicles, which at that time accounted for only 1 percent of Mack's sales. The announcement appeared in the Mack dealers' magazine, in an issue that contained a number of brief articles and pictures of newly delivered Macks. More dump trucks are pictured than any other body type.

Five dump trucks with twin rear axles sold by the Portland, Oregon, branch included two for the Northwest Natural Gas Company with Schenky bodies, two for the Clark County (Washington) Highway Department with Columbia bodies, and one to an owner-operator who designed his own dump body. The dealer in Montgomery, Alabama, sold a pair of Macks with triple rear axles and 18-yard Rogers dump bodies to a sand and gravel firm. The Mack dealer in Boston sold a Mack tractor to a sand hauler to pull a Raven 30-yard aluminum dump trailer between Middleboro and Martha's Vineyard and a dump body with snow plow attachment and all-wheel drive to the Medford (Massachusetts) Highway Department.

This is a 1971 International, pulling a pup trailer. *The Truck Gazette*

A 1971 Peterbilt with steel dump and transfer bodies built by Utility. *The Truck Gazette*

Left: This is an early 1970s Diamond-Reo with twin rear axles. *Mark R. Wayman*

Above: A Bartlett hydraulic-lifting fifth wheel. *Bartlett Trailer Corporation*

Left: A 1972 Dodge with twin rear axles and a Timpte dump body. *Mark R. Wayman*

An early 1970s Ford C with a dumping stake body installed by Earl Sherman Co. *Earl Sherman*

Right & Below: These 1972 photos show a Kress Carrier, operated by the Southwestern Illinois Coal Corporation. It could carry 150 tons. *National Coal Association*

Above: This is a 1972 Fargo (Canadian Dodge) with twin rear axles and a dump body. *The Truck Gazette*

Two Wabcos shown in a 1971 photo. Even the small one is big—compare it with the height of the spectator. *American Mining Congress*

The dump body on this 1973 Chevrolet could carry 2.2 yards. *The Truck Gazette*

Note raised wheel on this 1972 White Construcktor. These are often called "lift" axles and used only when the truck is loaded. *American Trucking Associations*

A 1970s GMC used on a U.S. Navy construction project. *Still Media Records Center, Department of Defense*

Chevrolet used this photo to promote its 1973 models. *American Trucking Associations*

Lectra Haul off-highway trucks were built in Tulsa. This picture shows two models from the early 1970s used in a copper mine. *American Mining Congress*

This new 1973 Dodge, with a dump body, sits in front of a dealer. Dodge dropped out of the large truck market in 1975. *The Truck Gazette*

Below: A circa 1973 Mack with side-dumping body at work on a road in South Carolina. South Carolina Department of *Highways and Public Transportation*

A 1973 Kenworth with a Challenge dump body. Wheels farthest to the rear are used only when the truck is loaded and are necessary to meet some state's weight and axle spacing requirements. When the truck is empty, the wheels are lifted upward, and carried in a raised position. *Kenworth Truck Co.*

An early 1970s Peterbilt with a Reliance body. *Mark R. Wayman*

C.C.C. trucks have been built by the Crane Carrier Corporation of Tulsa since 1953. The model, circa 1974, has a driver-only cab to the side of the engine. *The Truck Gazette*

Western Star trucks were associated with White and intended for West Coast markets, where more powerful trucks were often needed. This 1973 White Western Star has a dump body with a capacity of 10 to 12 yards. *The Truck Gazette*

Challenge-Cook Bros. built this off-highway earthmover in the mid-1970s. It's powered by a Caterpillar engine. *Challenge Cook Bros.*

This mid-1970s Diamond-Reo has a "lift" axle. *Mark R. Wayman*

This is a used 1974 Chevrolet for sale in San Jose. *The Truck Gazette*

A Galion 14-foot box on a 1974 Ford chassis. *The Truck Gazette*

This 1974 GMC has a dumping 18-foot flatbed body. *The Truck Gazette*

A mid-1970s Ford, being loaded with sand and grit to be spread on Kentucky highways. *Kentucky Department of Transportation*

This 1974 International was used in oil field construction on Alaska's north slope. It had a cold weather package that permitted it to operate in temperatures as cold as –65 degrees Fahrenheit. *Navistar*

A circa 1974 Mack in retirement. *Mark R. Wayman*

This is a mid-1970s Peterbilt truck with trailer. *Mark R. Wayman*

This Western Star is from the mid-1970s. *Mark R. Wayman*

A 1975 Chevrolet with twin rear axles and a large dump body. *The Truck Gazette*

Two mid-1970s Fords at work on a repaving project in South Carolina. *South Carolina Department of Highways and Public Transportation*

A mid-1970s Ford with a Peabody Galion body, dual axles, and a cab protector. *Peabody Galion*

This 1975 International has a Cook dump body and transfer trailer. *The Truck Gazette*

The 16-foot flatbed on this 1975 GMC is lifted by a twin-piston hoist. *The Truck Gazette*

The village of Lake Placid, New York, owns this mid-1970s GMC. It has a tarp on a roller to cover the load.

An Aristocrat dump body from the mid-1970s, built by the Truck Engineering Company of Fort Wayne. *The Truck Engineering Co.*

One type of fire apparatus is called a tanker, and most of them have the ability to "dump" water into a portable canvas tank, as shown here. The chassis is a 1976 Ford, operated by the Pittsville, Wisconsin, Fire Department. A second fire apparatus would pump water out of the temporary tank and use it to attack the fire. The empty tanker would then drive to the nearest hydrant or other water source and reload with water. (The tanker also carried a pump so it could draft from a lake or stream.) Square dumps like this can release water at a rate of over 1,000 gallons a minute. (Tankers on straight trucks carry 1,000 to 4,000 gallons.)
Dave Gitchell

A 1976 Ford dump truck with a crew cab and tool cabinets. *Earl Sherman*

This is an off-highway International "Payhauler," from the late 1970s. *American Mining Congress*

A Ford, circa 1977, with three rear axles and a Peabody Galion body lifted by a single piston. *Peabody Galion*

A Euclid from the late 1970s.
Mark R. Wayman

This 1977 White Road Boss has a 12-yard body. *The Truck Gazette*

This is a 1979 GMC General with a 10- to 12-yard dump body. *The Truck Gazette*

A late 1970s Diamond-Reo truck with full trailer and a total of 10 axles. *Western Reserve Library*

A 10-yard Columbia dump body on a 1980 International chassis. *The Truck Gazette*

Plymouth has produced light trucks on a sporadic basis. This is a 1979 Plymouth Arrow, which was built by Mitsubishi and sold by Chrysler/Plymouth dealers. The dump body was built by Thiele. Even with dual rear tires, the rig's weight-carrying capacity would be low. *Thiele, Inc.*

This 1979 International has an 8- to 10-yard Newell body. *The Truck Gazette*

A circa 1980 Peterbilt tractor with a Flow Boy semitrailer, which is unloaded horizontally toward the rear by use of a chain conveyor. Unloading time was less than one minute for some commodities. The units could also carry hot mix, or could be operated with a spreader at the rear. *Flow Boy*

Chapter 9

1981–Present

A Dump Truck for Every Purpose

The products of Thiele, Inc., of Winther, Pennsylvania, give an idea of the marketplace in the early 1980s. Thiele built and sold hydraulic pumps and about 20 different underbody hoists with capacities ranging between 1 and 50 tons. Its smallest bodies were built to fit the "compact" trucks of the time: Chevy Luv, Datsun, Ford Courier, Mazda, and Toyota. Actually two sizes were offered, one holding 1 yard, the other, 1-1/4 yards. The hoist for the smaller body was rated at 1 ton, the larger body's hoist was rated at 2 tons. For 1-ton pickups, Thiele offered a dump body that fit inside the pickup box. The hoist was at the front of the dump box and powered by 12-volt current. Another body replaced the pickup body on 1/2-ton and 3/4-ton trucks. Several bodies were offered at 2-yard capacity, and they look like the size used by municipalities for many tasks (except plowing snow).

The next size Thiele dump bodies held from 3 to 5 yards and were the largest used on chassis with a single rear axle. Some of these bodies were sufficiently high that they came equipped with a ladder in the left front corner. Options on these bodies included a revolving light, a pintle hook, and a back-up alarm. The next size

An early 1980s C.C.C. sold to the U.S. Army. It has three rear axles. *American Automobile Manufacturers Assn.*

of Thiele bodies were intended for chassis with two or three rear axles—for the latter, Thiele offered to sell and install the third axle assembly. These very large bodies were available in either steel or aluminum. Also available were three models of dumping semitrailers carried on twin axles. Thiele also sold three sizes of "semipup" trailers. They rode on two axles and had a relatively long tongue—apparently designed with axle weight and spacing regulations in mind. The final Thiele bodies were for tree trimmers, and one carried a "cherry picker" device to lift the trimmer. Behind this was a large enclosed body for trimmings that could be dumped. Its hoist was powered by the same system that powered the cherry picker.

The Tesco high-lift body, built in Fort Lauderdale, used a scissors-lift to elevate a horizontal body, such as those used to lift catered meals into large aircraft. The horizontal body could be ordered with a dump feature, so that it could be raised and then dumped. (Some coal bodies built in the 1920s and 1930s operated in a similar manner.)

Towing services began switching from conventional tow trucks to tilt bed trucks with flat bodies, the rear end of which could be lowered to the ground. The recovered vehicle would then be winched onto the bed and the bed restored to level. These rigs increased in use because the new auto bumpers that were designed to absorb front-end impacts often could not be lifted by a tow truck's conventional equipment.

A 1990 brochure for the Terex articulated dump truck shows how far these large off-road vehicles had developed. The tractor had one axle and was permanently coupled to a two-axle trailer, and all axles were powered. The engine was a Cummins diesel. It had no tailgate but the rear of the body was shaped like a chute, at a 25-degree angle. The body's floor and tailchute were made of steel .51 inches thick; the front and lower

This is a 1981 Chevrolet C50 with a Thiele dump body. *Thiele Industries, Inc.*

sides were .39 inches thick, and the upper sides were .31 inches thick. The payload was 30 tons. The hoist could lift the loaded body to 65 degree in 13 seconds, and lower it in 9 seconds. The cab has both roll-over and falling object protection and a roof ventilator that also served as an escape hatch. (The Terex home office was in Scotland with the U.S. subsidiary located in Hudson, Ohio.)

In 1999, as this book was being written, the author made several forays onto the World Wide Web looking for materials on dump trucks. About 70 entries were listed, mainly body builders or installers, or used truck or used truck body dealers. There were also 43 firms listed as members of the National Truck Equipment Association's technical section dealing with dump bodies and conversion hoists. There was some overlap in the two lists. A few old names that appeared on these lists included Galion, Heil, Knapheide, Omaha Standard, and Schwartz. The search also uncovered accessories and attachments for dump bodies, including a chute for filling sandbags (in flood situations), underbody stabilizers, tailgates that both swing and can lift to and from the ground, spreaders, body liners, tarp systems, and chipper bodies.

Business Trucking magazine's November 1999 issue had two articles dealing with dump trucks. One concerned northern California's Siskiyou County and how county officials "spec'd" (specified) the 10-yard dump trucks they purchased to plow snow in the winter and haul construction materials year-round. Virgil Hardy, the county's fleet supervisor, said that the county originally piggybacked on state truck fleet orders but "we usually got underpowered vehicles . . . . They were spec'd for the flat lands and didn't have the horsepower to haul a trailer or a sander and plow up in the mountains. In the end, it took two of those trucks to do the same job that just one of the new ones does." Presently the county buys Kenworths with Caterpillar diesels, 13-speed transmissions, front and rear axle load boosters, and heavy-duty front axles (for the snow plows). Most have towing hitches. Aluminum cabs are used because they are less easily corroded and save weight. The engines produce between 415 and 435 horsepower and are expected to last between 500,000 and 550,000 miles. The cabs have AM/FM radios, air conditioning, air-ride seats, and power windows. Each is assigned to a different driver.

An early 1980s Chevrolet with a crew cab and small dump body. It's outfitted with rail wheels, and was used by a construction company. *Mark R. Wayman*

Twin rear axles and a large dump box on a 1982 Ford chassis. *The Truck Gazette*

An early 1980s Ford with three rear axles, feeding a paving machine in South Carolina. *South Carolina Department of Highways and Public Transportation*

The second article dealt with a firm named Red Walker Trucking that operates a dump fleet and sells trucks and other equipment in South Carolina. Jerry McNeill, who works for the firm, said that heavier-duty specs are necessary for dump trucks. "Our customers want specially equipped vehicles they can't find on the dealer lot, like big power, double frames, longer wheelbases, and larger rear axles." They have worked with Hendrickson Suspension Systems to develop new suspension beams that are as strong as, but lighter than, conventional suspension beams. Reduced weight allows for increased payload. Finding good drivers is a challenge. "We try to attract and keep the best ones by making the cab as comfortable as possible, with air conditioning and power seats—you name it. With our 130 drivers riding in a truck worth more than

$100,000, they should be happy with it and so take care of it. That is especially important when it comes time to sell the used equipment."

For 100 years, the dump truck has played an important role in virtually all major construction projects, military operations and many important industries. Interestingly, the actual dump truck technology has changed little over this long span of years. Two improvements that cannot be detected from photos are better linkages between the truck engine and the hoist, and steel that is lighter in weight but more resistant to abrasions. Dump bodies last longer and are more likely to be switched from an older chassis to a newer one.

In the twenty-first century we can expect to recognize dump trucks at work, with the only obvious change being that they may become even bigger.

This early 1980s Autocar had a Thiele dump body. *Thiele Industries, Inc.*

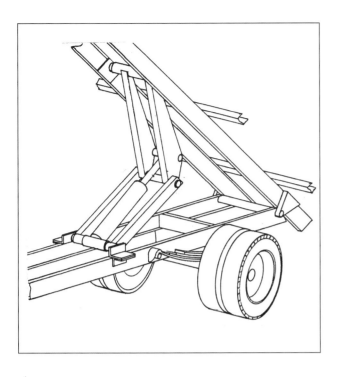

These drawings, which appeared in some Crysteel literature in the early 1980s, showed several different types of hydraulic hoists.

Left: This is a scissors hoist with the thrust driving the arms apart, in an action similar to forcing a pair of closed scissors open. *Crysteel Mfg. Inc.; reproduced with permission*

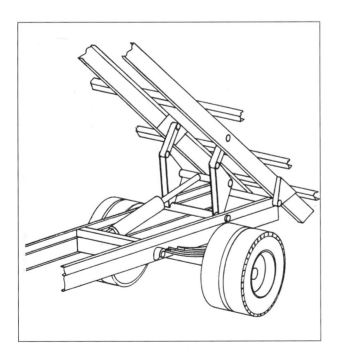

This is a double arm that pushes back under the body, raising it. It rides under the body and usually is mounted closer to the rear, when compared to the scissors hoist. *Crysteel Mfg. Inc.; reproduced with permission*

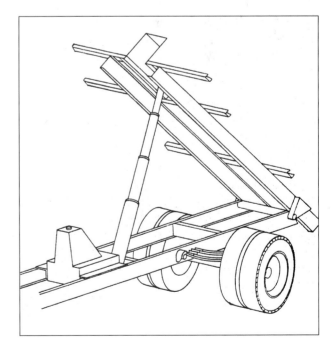

This is the telescopic hoist mounted at the front of the body. Sometimes a "dog-house" is used to contain the closed telescope inside the lowered body. *Crysteel Mfg. Inc.; reproduced with permission*

Close-up view of two Fruehauf bottom-dump trailers. Each could carry 11 yards of material. *Fruehauf*

This is an early 1980s Chevrolet dump pulling a flatbed trailer that carries a Caterpillar wheeled tractor. The truck was owned by the Santa Fe Railroad. The diamond-shaped brackets on the front grille and side of the dump body are used when carrying hazardous materials placards. *Mark R. Wayman*

This system allows a body to function as a dump body or to be deposited onto (or lifted from) the ground. The system was from Prentek Corporation of Prentice, Wisconsin; the truck is a small Chevrolet. *Prentek Corporation*

Here's how dump bodies are carried. These five on a flatbed trailer appeared in a trade journal ad from a dealer who had "20 new 10-to-12-yard dump boxes." *The Truck Gazette*

A 1982 Ford with a 5-yard box, on a used truck lot in Sacramento. *The Truck Gazette*

THIELE
ALUMINUM DUMP BODY

CHECK THESE THIELE QUALITY FEATURES

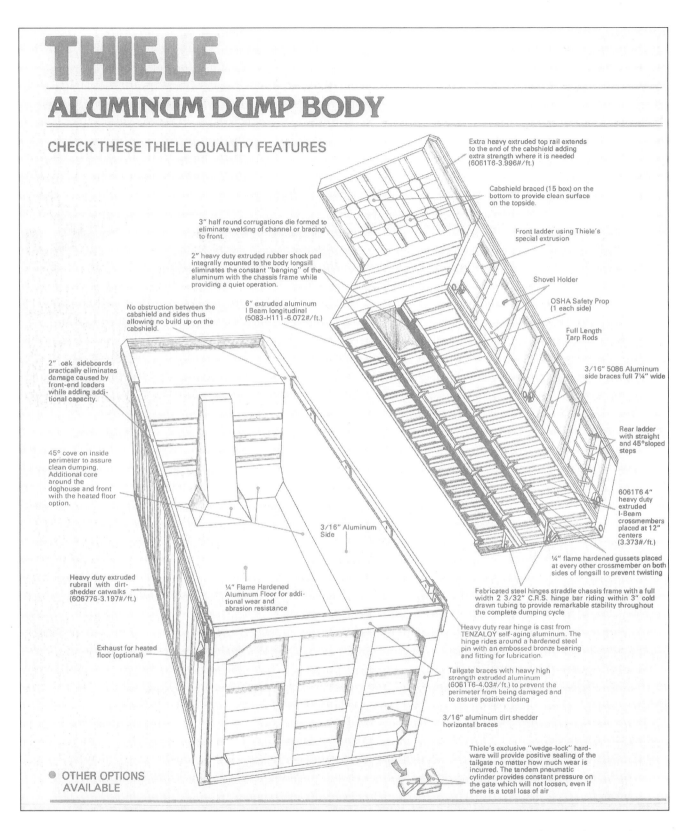

Extra heavy extruded top rail extends to the end of the cabshield adding extra strength where it is needed (6061T6-3.996#/ft.)

Cabshield braced (15 box) on the bottom to provide clean surface on the topside.

Front ladder using Thiele's special extrusion

Shovel Holder

OSHA Safety Prop (1 each side)

Full Length Tarp Rods

3/16" 5086 Aluminum side braces full 7¼" wide

Rear ladder with straight and 45°sloped steps

6061T6 4" heavy duty extruded I-Beam crossmembers placed at 12" centers (3.373#/ft.)

¼" flame hardened gussets placed at every other crossmember on both sides of longsill to prevent twisting

3" half round corrugations die formed to eliminate welding of channel or bracing to front.

2" heavy duty extruded rubber shock pad integrally mounted to the body longsill eliminates the constant "banging" of the aluminum with the chassis frame while providing a quiet operation.

No obstruction between the cabshield and sides thus allowing no build up on the cabshield.

6" extruded aluminum I Beam longitudinal (5083-H111-6.072#/ft.)

2" oak sideboards practically eliminates damage caused by front-end loaders while adding additional capacity.

45° cove on inside perimeter to assure clean dumping. Additional core around the doghouse and front with the heated floor option.

3/16" Aluminum Side

Heavy duty extruded rubrail with dirt-shedder catwalks (606776-3.197#/ft.)

¼" Flame Hardened Aluminum Floor for additional wear and abrasion resistance

Exhaust for heated floor (optional)

Fabricated steel hinges straddle chassis frame with a full width 2 3/32" C.R.S. hinge bar riding within 3" cold drawn tubing to provide remarkable stability throughout the complete dumping cycle

Heavy duty rear hinge is cast from TENZALOY self-aging aluminum. The hinge rides around a hardened steel pin with an embossed bronze bearing and fitting for lubrication.

Tailgate braces with heavy high strength extruded aluminum (6061T6-4.03#/ft.) to prevent the perimeter from being damaged and to assure positive closing

3/16" aluminum dirt shedder horizontal braces

Thiele's exclusive "wedge-lock" hardware will provide positive sealing of the tailgate no matter how much wear is incurred. The tandem pneumatic cylinder provides constant pressure on the gate which will not loosen, even if there is a total loss of air

● OTHER OPTIONS AVAILABLE

This drawing of a Thiele body appeared in some of the firm's 1982 literature. The hoist lifts nearly straight up in the front of the body; note area built around it. *Thiele Industries, Inc.*

This 1983 Kenworth carries a 15-foot-long Williamson dump body. *The Truck Gazette*

In 1999 a Phase II dump body, built in Glade Spring, Virginia, was installed on this 1985 Autocar chassis with four rear axles, the front two being "lift axles" that are raised when the truck is empty. The body will be used for carrying gravel and asphalt. Note rod leaning forward in the center of the body. It holds the tarpaulin that can be placed on top of the load. The mechanism holding the rod is spring-loaded so it snaps into place either forward or rearward. *Phase II Truck Body*

This 1985 GMC General has a 10-yard Williamson dump body. *The Truck Gazette*

We see here a mid-1980s Kenworth dump truck with four axles pulling a three-axle trailer. *Mark R. Wayman*

This 1986 Mack carries a 10-yard Williamson dump body. *The Truck Gazette*

A late 1980s Navistar International operated by Pacific Gas & Electric Company, a California utility. It has a Heil dump body. *Mark R. Wayman*

This is a 1988 RTI, built in Chino, California. Different compartments are for handling segregated recyclables. *Refuse News Archives*

Marmon trucks, descendents of Marmon-Herrington, are assembled in Garland, Texas. *Mark R. Wayman*

These bottom-dump semi and full trailers are enclosed to carry a product that must be protected from the elements. Truck tractor is a circa 1990 Peterbilt. *Mark R. Wayman*

This is a circa 1990 Peterbilt with a dump body and a transfer dump trailer. *Mark R. Wayman*

This is a mid-1990s Lectra Haul off-highway dump truck. *Mark R. Wayman*

This is the front of a transfer trailer. The grille covers a battery-operated motor that is used to pull the transfer trailer's box in and out of the truck's box. The battery is charged by the truck when the truck and trailer are linked. *Reliance*

Here is a massive dumping trailer device pulled by an early 1990s Kenworth semitractor. *The Truck Gazette*

The 1990 Ford was spotted in Saranac Lake, New York. The sides of the dump body have been built up with boards to accommodate a bulk load, such as trimmed brush.

This is a Reliance transfer trailer. In front of the box we see a bicycle-style chain that moves the box forward. On the bottom we see that the tongue has been dropped to the ground. At the front of the trailer are two "horns" that must be married to two openings in the rear of the truck. The chain moves the trailer's box forward into the truck's box and a cog at the end of the chain pushes into the truck's box where it is secured before it is dumped. *Reliance*

This is an early 1990s Freightliner with a Fontaine dump body. The rod on the side of the body is for a tarpaulin. *Freightliner*

This mid-1990s Kenworth tractor is pulling one semi and two full bottom-dump trailers. *Mark R. Wayman*

Here's a Terex earth hauler. The manufacturer is located in Tulsa. *Mark R. Wayman*

CALTRANS, the California transportation agency, operates this 1995 GMC. Currently it's carrying a plastic tank used for spraying along the roadside. The device in the far rear drops into a horizontal position when the truck is parked or operating at low speeds. Its purpose is to cushion the impact of a rear-end crash. The truck has a radio and just behind the cab is a speaker so crews working outside the truck can hear. Above the cab is a sign that, when in a vertical position, can display messages.

A 1995 Ford with twin rear axles has just dumped a load of dirt in a street repair project in Saranac Lake, New York.

This Volvo dump truck is from the mid-1990s. It has rail wheels as well as highway tires. *Mark R. Wayman*

A Peterbilt dump truck pulling two transfer trailers for use in Nevada. The two trailers are kept linked—the truck takes the front one from the front and the rear one from the rear. *Reliance*

This is a mid-1990s Navistar International with a Heil dump body, and automatic top cover. *Mark R. Wayman*

A Reliance transfer rig, showing the trailer's box as it moves into the truck's box. It must be secured, and the truck moved away from the trailer chassis, before it can be dumped. A skilled driver can dump a transfer truck and trailer in seven minutes. *Reliance*

This is a late 1990s Peterbilt with a Reliance body and booster axles in raised position. *Reliance*

A late 1990s Stahl body on a medium-size GMC chassis, with a tarp on the roller at the top. Stahl is located in Wooster, Ohio, where it was founded in 1946. *Stahl*

Bibliography

Allhands, J. L. *Tools of the Earth Mover, Yesterday and Today, Preserved in Pictures.* Huntsville, Texas: Sam Houston College Press, 1951.

Anthony Company literature, 1945–1955.

Appelquist, Harlan E. "American Truck Builders of 1939," *The Bulb Horn* (March–April 1974), 30–33.

Baker Equipment Engineering Company Catalog, circa 1930.

Bartlett Trailer Corporation literature, circa 1975.

Bracher, Eric. "The History of the Linn Tractor," *Timber Times*, issue 20 (circa 1998), 10–11.

Burness, Tad. *American Truck & Bus Spotter's Guide 1920–1985.* Osceola, Wisconsin: MBI Publishing Company, 1985.

Business Trucking, November 1999.

Challenge-Cook literature, early 1980s.

Clement Industries literature, circa 1978.

Commercial Shearing & Stamping Co. literature, 1928, 1931.

Crismon, Fred W. *International Trucks.* Osceola, Wisconsin: MBI Publishing Company, 1995.

Crysteel Mfg. Inc. literature, 1980s and 1990s.

Cummins Powered Euclid Equipment. Cleveland: The Euclid Road Machinery Co., 1953.

Dart literature, 1983.

Dependable Diesel, The (a Cummins Engine Company periodical), various issues, 1946–1954.

Detroit Automotive Products literature, circa 1948.

Detroit Trailer Company price list, 1922.

Ditwiler Manufacturing Company literature, circa 1927.

"Dump Bodies Advance with Truck Design," *The Commercial Car Journal* (April 1930), 38–41.

Dunham Manufacturing Co. literature, circa 1980.

"Electric Vehicles in Coal Haulage," *The Motor Truck* (October 1912), 650–654.

Energy Hydraulics Manufacturing Co. literature, circa 1965.

Flow Boy literature, circa 1980.

Freeman Truck Bodies, Inc. literature, circa 1975.

Frink Snow Plow literature, 1939.

FWD NEWS, circa 1968.

Galion Sales Suggestions, 1955.

Gar Wood literature, circa 1939.

Heil Co. literature, 1930s and 1940s.

Henderson literature, 1990s.

Hercules Dump Body literature, circa 1928.

Hobbs Trailers literature, circa 1975.

Homemade Rubber Tired Wagons and Trailers. Brookings, South Dakota: Agricultural Experiment Station, 1941.

"Hydraulic Hoists and Dumping Bodies," *Transportation Engineering Bulletins*, Packard Motor Car Co., no. 5, June 10, 1920.

Hydraulics Unlimited Mfg. Co. literature, circa 1980.

Interboro Hoist and Body Corp. literature, 1926.

Isaacson Truck Equipment literature, 1930s.

Lectra Haul literature, 1960s.

Lindgren, C. W. *Automotive and Construction Equipment.* Washington, D.C.: (self-published), 1951.

Little Giant Products literature, 1946–1948.

Mack Trucks, Earth Moving and Hauling of Building and Road Materials. New York: International Motor Company, circa 1921.

Mack Steel Dump Bodies, net price list. New York: International Motor Company, circa 1924.

Mack Bulldog (first quarter 1979).

Martin-Parry body literature, 1926–1929.

Martin-Parry Company. *Fifty Vocations and How to Sell Them.* York, Pennsylvania: (published by the company), 1928.

McMillan, A. G. *Model A/AA Ford Truck Owner* (a compilation of loose-leaf binder pages distributed to Ford dealers, circa 1930). Arcadia, California: Post-Era Books, 1975.

Mid West Body literature, circa 1950–1960.

Motor Truck at the Coal Mines. Akron: Firestone Ship By Truck Bureau, 1920.

"Motor Truck Dealers Make Good Profits by Selling Standardized Truck Bodies With Chassis," *The Commercial Car Journal* (June 15, 1919), 31–50.

Mroz, Albert. *The Illustrated Encyclopedia of American Trucks and Commercial Vehicles.* Iola, Wisconsin: Krause, 1996.

Municipal Index, 8th edition. New York: *American City Magazine*, 1931.

Municipal Index, 24th edition. New York: *American City Magazine*, 1950.

National Truck Equipment Company literature, circa 1950.

Norton, S. V. *The Motor Truck as an Aid to Business Profits.* Chicago: A. W. Shaw, 1918.

Page, Victor W. *The Modern Motor Truck.* New York: Henley, 1921.

Peabody Galion literature, circa 1977.

Penn Body literature, circa 1941.

Pierce-Arrow truck literature, 1924.

Refuse Collection Equipment. Chicago: American Public Works Association, 1940.

Reliance literature, 1990s.

Rock Manufacturing Company literature, circa 1930.

Schien Body and Equipment Co. literature, circa 1980.

Special Bodies on the Speed Wagon Chassis. Lansing: Reo Motor Car Company, 1922.

Springfield Commercial Bodies especially designed for Chevrolet chassis, 1926.

Sternberg, Ernest. *A History of Motor Truck Development.* Warrendale, Pennsylvania: Society of Automotive Engineers, 1981.

Terex literature, 1990.

Tesco literature, circa 1982.

Thiele, Inc. literature, 1981.

Twin City Motor Truck 2-ton and 3-1/2-ton literature, circa 1921.

Truck Inventory and Use Survey, 1967 Census of Transportation. Washington, D.C.: Bureau of the Census, 1969.

"Truck Trailer Shipments & Percentage of Total by Type, 1954–1969." Washington, D.C.: Truck Trailer Manufacturers Association, circa 1970.

Twenty Years' Progress in Commercial Motor Vehicles. Detroit: Automotive Council for War Production, 1942.

United Automotive Body Company literature, circa 1920.

U.S. 3-Way Hoist & Body literature, 1928.

Warren literature, 1990s.

Weltman, W. C. "Welding an Aluminum Dump Body," *The Welding Journal* (January 1956).

Wren, James A., and Genevieve J. Wren, *Motor Trucks of America.* Ann Arbor, Michigan: University of Michigan Press, 1979.

Index